AF478333

Acquired Taste

Food and the Art of Consumption

OCTOBER 29 - DECEMBER 11, 2011

BEGOVICH GALLERY, CSU FULLERTON

Curated by Alyssa Cordova & Heather Richards-Siddons

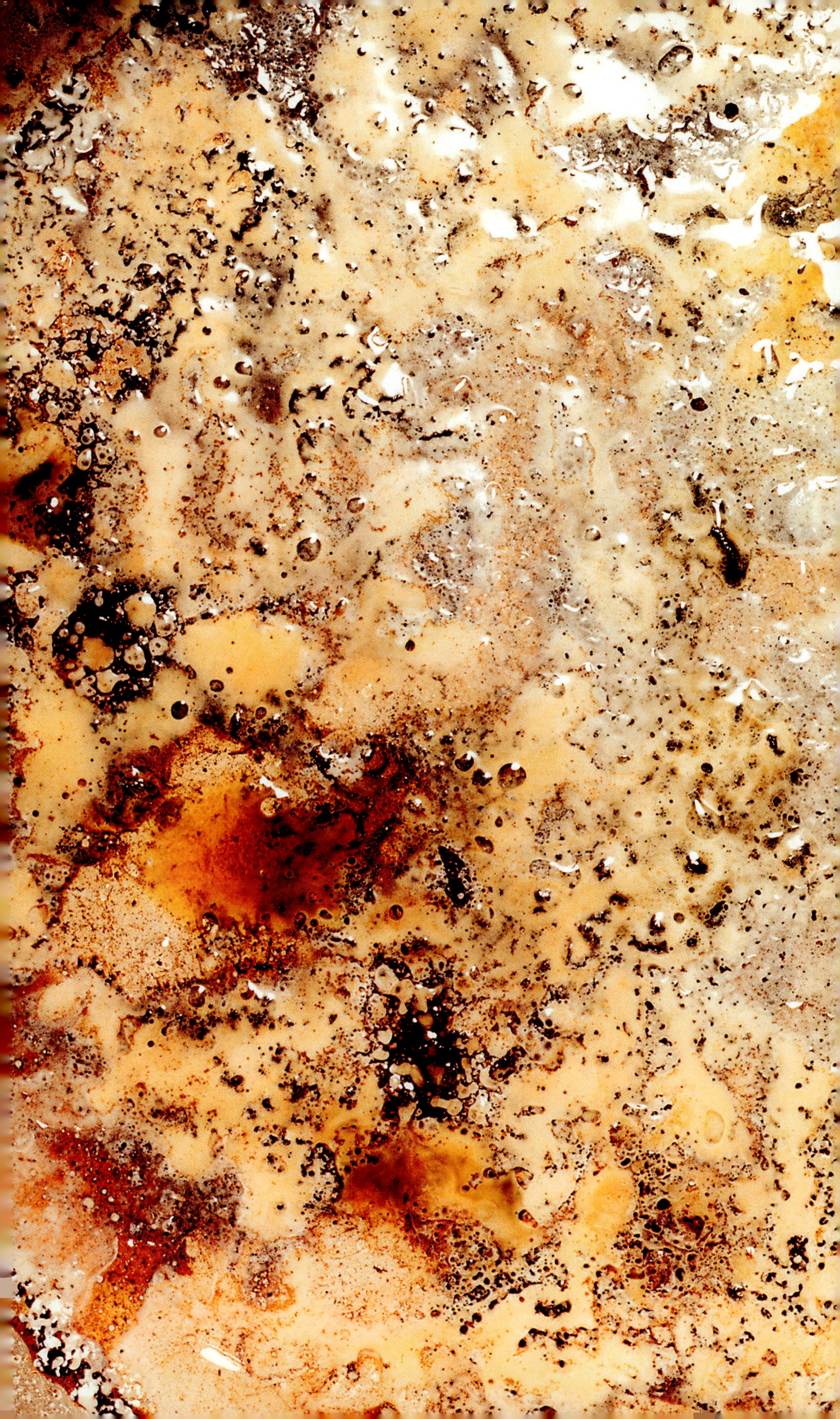

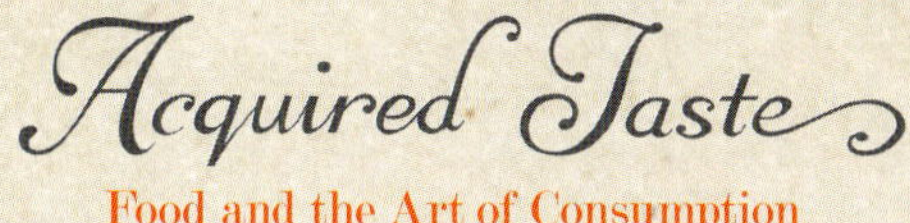

Food and the Art of Consumption

CONTENTS

*Denotes recipes

FOREWORD

Mike McGee

Director, Nicholas & Lee Begovich Gallery

Food, of course, is a necessity. It isn't until we get beyond the basic needs for survival that we have the luxury of cultivating food as an acquired taste. And, although some might argue that art is a necessity for the soul, it too—particularly contemporary art—is an acquired taste.

This project, *Acquired Taste: Food and the Art of Consumption*, is essentially about the intersection of these two acquired tastes. As several of the writers for this publication have mentioned, the depiction of food in art has a long and storied history. Some of the oldest prehistoric cave paintings depict images of the animals our ancestors hunted for food. Nicole J. Caruth points out in her thoughtful essay for this publication that there is a direct correlation between our collective relationship to food and its treatment by artists.

Although it is difficult to accurately quantify evidence for such a claim, it seems to me just from anecdotal observation that more artists today are making art about food than in any other period in history. I believe this heightened interest reflects growing recognition of and discourse about the connections between food and socioeconomic factors and realities. In the United States our relationship with food has, in recent years, become a mortally critical issue. After a half-century of eating unprecedented high levels of processed foods, salt, sugar, fat, and red meat, we are confronting the toll our diet is taking on our health, with heart disease and diabetes at the top of a long list of resulting maladies.

In any event, in their preliminary research for this project, curators Alyssa Cordova and Heather Richards amassed a substantial list of artists for consideration. Their early challenge was to establish criteria to narrow the list to the thirteen artists in this exhibition. All the artists in the exhibition in some way or another address or allude to the issues I outlined above. But the first impression here is visual: bold minimal elements, decorative flourishes, pop art devices, and just plain curious imagery pull you into these artworks. Once you get there, your engagement is sustained with visceral subject matter, textures, tastes, and even smells. Just beyond that are the ideas and concepts that make this project so compelling.

I commend Cordova and Richards for their perseverance in bringing together a group of artists whose works collectively form such a cohesive and thought-provoking statement. I also want to thank the writers and the artists who participated in this project, many of whom put forth extraordinary effort to make work especially for this exhibition. I also want to acknowledge the Cal State Fullerton graphic design student designers who designed this publication. And, finally, I want to extend a special thank you to Williams-Sonoma chef and culinary instructor Jonathan Dye. His recipes corresponding to the artworks and cooking demonstration at the exhibition reception brought the project full circle by adding a tasty reminder as to what this project is about: *food.*

CURATORS' STATEMENT

Alyssa Cordova &
Heather Richards-Siddons

We do it three or more times a day with our hands and mouths in a coordinated fluidity of movement—sometimes with careful planning and artistry; other times mindlessly and on the go; sometimes as a personal, guilty pleasure, or other times in celebration with others: We consume food.

Eating is not merely biological, it also intertwines cultures, regions, and generations. Passed down over centuries, food is a type of storytelling. It traces migratory movements and underscores the cross-cultural fusion of people to place. Food also connotes social status, oftentimes unabashedly proclaiming one's allegiance to country or class, or in a broader sense, taste. Food historian Massimo Montanari argues, "Taste is a cultural product, not, in fact, subjective and incommunicable, but rather collective and eminently communicative; we learn or adopt an 'acquired taste' through exposure and experience."

We have a reciprocal relationship to food: we consume it and it consumes us by infiltrating nearly every aspect of our lives. Each of the artists selected for *Acquired Taste* envisions food not merely as substance but as an extension of ourselves; perhaps we really are what we eat.

Bon Appétit!

ESSAYS

BRINGING ART TO THE TABLE

Alyssa Cordova

Curator

He who eats alone chokes alone. — proverb

Feasting and the rituals humans create surrounding food consumption distinguish us from other creatures of the animal kingdom. Humans do more than consume food for sustenance; we *experience* it, and we do so collectively. Food archeologist Martin Jones writes, "The shared meal remains a very central feature in our social lives, a marker of who our friends and relations are and what it is to be human." Which begs the question: is it the food itself or the shared experience that ties us together? For some people, food can even be a simulacrum for relationship, a common denominator pervasive in our personal narrative. The dinner table transforms into a metaphor for community.

While we are likely familiar with art that portrays food and the rituals associated with it, such as Giuseppe Arcimboldi's food portraits or Leonardo da Vinci's *The Last Supper,* in recent decades contemporary artists have begun to explore our collective relationship to food and the implications of those relationships to our communities through participatory components. In her 1979 installation *The Dinner Party,* feminist artist Judy Chicago used unoccupied place settings at an elaborate meal to symbolize and pay homage to famous women of myth and history. In the early 1990s, artist Felix Gonzalez-Torres used familiar sweets in his candy-spill installations, such as *Untitled (Portrait of Ross in L.A.)* of 1991, in which viewers were invited to help themselves to pieces of candy during their exhibition visit. More recently, trends in popular culture indicate a growing general interest in the culinary arts: food has become the guest of honor at our meals. This trend has begun to influence visual art in ways that Chicago and Gonzalez-Torres may never have envisioned.

Building on the associations between food and human relationship represented in these famous works of art, the exhibition *Acquired Taste: Food and the Art of Consumption* brings together thirteen contemporary artists whose visual commentary directly addresses our complex relationship to food and ultimately with one another. Four of the artists examine the meal as a space for facilitating community and shared experience. Their work here includes a multimedia installation by Shannon Hayes Faseler; a conversation brought to life by Jennifer Knox through the pages of an altered cookbook; and the still-life paintings of Pamela Johnson and a community mural project by Tattfoo Tan, which examine gastronomy in the context of American culture.

Socially, to sit down at a table and partake of a meal with others usually means acceptance into a specific group, perhaps even a family. Similarly, with installation art, viewers engage in a collaborative, unified action by experiencing an interactive space together. In the installation *Aesthetics of Decay*, 2011, Shannon Faseler has fabricated a life-size, realistic, domestic parlor reminiscent of the New Orleans Victorian-era homes destroyed by Hurricane Katrina. A stop-motion animation video of slowly growing mold spores is projected onto hand-painted wallpaper. As viewers stand in the ten-by-ten foot room watching the animated mold, they are virtually transported to a familiar shared moment in time: when the American people came together during the aftermath of Katrina. By physically entering the space, we also become participants in the slow, beautiful, but ultimately destructive decay of an environment confronting the temporal nature of time, place, and food.

Jennifer Knox's *Altered Cookbook* reminds us to preserve community through cooking together. Dialog and food preparation often go hand in hand. Many memorable, tender, and revealing moments have likely occurred as individuals converse while preparing food and eating a meal together. In many ways, the meal itself can be broken down to components similar to the syntax of language. Food historian Massimo Montanari writes, on the grammar of food, "Rhetoric is the adaptation of speech to the argument, to the effects one wants to arouse or create. If the discourse is food, that means the way in which it is prepared, served and eaten."[1] Knox's work comments on notions of authorship and identity and is both object and performance: She pastes personal letters and stories addressed to her friends directly over author Mark Bittman's writings, and then gives the defaced book as a wedding present. Knox supplants the generic, impersonal text of the best-selling cookbook with her own intimate and autobiographical writing. *Altered Cookbook* invites a relationship with viewers: as they partake of Knox's personal narrative, they ingest it into their psyches as if it were actually edible.

Contents of our meals have recently emerged as a significant focus in the conversation between food and art. In their time, seventeenth-century Dutch still-life paintings of food conveyed notions of agriculture, opulence, and refined taste; current audiences view these same works as historical documents about the diets, feasting rituals, and social classes of the period, while still appreciating the paintings for their artistic significance.

Still-life painting continues to be a genre for developing a gastronomical identity. The contemporary still lifes by Pamela Johnson in *Acquired Taste* address our current relationship with food and its consumption. Johnson's detailed oil painting *Gummi Bears* depicts a solitary, half-empty, spilled bag of the popular candy against a stark, midnight-blue background. Johnson's beautiful, honest, and simplistic image reflects current trends in eating. Like the work of her Dutch predecessors, Johnson's depiction of uninspired processed food far removed from the natural ingredients used to create it will likely become an anthropological artifact of American history. "It is the act of painting [objects in still lifes] that makes them perennially poised, an emergent truth about to be articulated, a word waiting to be spoken," remarks writer Mark Doty on the mysteries of still-life painting.[2] Johnson's work prompts viewers to contemplate the sources of our food and the layers of meaning in consumption.

While Johnson's paintings capture the stark truth about American eating practices in hope that we might mend our processed ways, Tattfoo Tan's *Nature Matching System* offers suggestions through his work that involves members of the community. America is a civilization of consumers, and what we eat and how we should eat are topics recently explored by authors and artists alike. Best-selling journalist Michael Pollan addresses the growing complexity of our consumption, writing, "As a culture we seem to have arrived at a place where whatever native wisdom we may have once possessed about eating has been replaced by confusion and anxiety."[3] Oftentimes we eat not even knowing what we are eating or where it came from. Tattfoo Tan's collaborative murals involve entire communities, schools, and children who paint samples of the natural colors of edible plants, ranging from the vibrant pink of a turnip to the shades of avocado green. Tan and the volunteer artists of *Nature Matching System* create a playful, visual reminder to return to natural and healthy forms of consumption. As participants work on a creative solution together, their exchanges often emulate the problem-solving process of a productive conversation around the dinner table.

Acquired Taste: Food and the Art of Consumption offers a community of visual artists interested in creating a dialog with viewers about food consumption. Whether by the unification of participants through installation art, cooking together, or exploring how we as a culture consume food, the works in this exhibition suggest ways we can better understand our complicated relationship with food and with each other.

[1] Martin Jones, *Feast: Why Humans Share Food* (Oxford: Oxford University Press, 2007), 8.
[2] Massimo Montanari, *Food is Culture* (New York: Columbia University Press, 2006), 102.
[3] Mark Doty, *Still Life with Oysters and Lemon* (Boston: Beacon Press, 2011), 18.
[4] Michael Pollan, *The Omnivore's Dilemma: A Natural History of Four Meals* (London: Penguin Books, 2006), 2, 411.

MAKING A ROUX: PERFORMING IDENTITY IN THE KITCHEN

Heather Richards-Siddons

Curator

Food is our common ground, a universal experience. — James Beard

As culinary experts and at-home chefs know, it all begins with a roux—melted butter cooked together with flour to create a thickening agent. Roux is the basis of three out of the five "mother sauces" in the classic French cook's arsenal: béchamel, espagnole, and *sauce tomate*. It is also the home chef's secret weapon, acting as the foundation of any wonderfully rich sauce. Without a roux, the food that comforts us would be inconceivable: there would be no gumbo, no biscuits and white gravy, and certainly no macaroni and cheese. Similarly, the performative ritual of cooking can be understood as a roux of a different kind, one that binds our self-image to our family structure. In *Acquired Taste: Food and the Art of Consumption*, the intersections of identity, food, and family are explored in the work of artists Sita Kuratomi Bhaumik and Mary Parisi. Installation artist Sita Kuratomi Bhaumik taps into her Southeast Asian, Japanese, and Colombian roots to create an immersive experience that engages one of the most powerful senses—our sense of smell. Mary Parisi's food photographs, drawing upon her memories of cooking with her father, powerfully highlight the strange beauty and often disquieting brutality associated with food.

We are what we eat. Or so we have been told by generations of mothers longing to see their children finish their vegetables. However cliché, this truism finds a basis not in the traditional concept of "eating all your food groups," but in the theory that identity is, in part, constructed through the ritual of cooking. In the kitchen, social roles and family history are played out, observed, and reenacted by later generations, binding action to identity in what Erving Goffman describes as a performance of self. The construction of one's identity through the kitchen is as much an extension of nurtured traits as it is an aspirational fantasy in which we create an idealized version of ourselves through performance. For children, this can take the

"

form of gendered play where family roles are mimicked; "playing house," for example, acts out traditional caretaker roles such as child rearing and cooking. For adults, the "kitchen fantasy" is driven most notably by television cooking shows, which offer viewers glamorous facsimiles of kitchens where pots and pans are always gleaming and every ingredient, condiment, and finished recipe is ready for its closeup. We participate in this fantasy by purchasing the goods and foodstuffs showcased, attempting to approximate Ina Garten's elegant, earthy Westhampton lifestyle or the verve and gusto of Mario Batali's rustic Italian cooking. By "performing" this idealized self, we convey who we are or who we long to be.

Writer Barbara Kirshenblatt-Gimblett frames the quotidian activity of cooking within the construct of performance, identifying three critical points where they converge: the production and presentation of food, etiquette and codified social graces surrounding food and eating, and the evaluation and appreciation of food, where the sense "taste" and the aesthetic "taste" meet.[1] Many artists working within the performative genre have used food, cooking, and the kitchen to engage the viewer's sense of self in relation to others. In 1964, Allan Kaprow staged his performance *Eat* in a series of abandoned caves on the site of the former Ebling Brewery in the Bronx, New York. Guests wandered through the connected caves for a one-hour period and interacted (or not) with staged vignettes, including performers cooking and edible food installations. Later, Gordon Matta-Clark co-opened *Food*, a conceptual restaurant where artist-chefs created food that was frequently inedible but nonetheless entertaining. One performative dinner featured an all-bone menu with such offerings as oxtail, frogs' legs, and bone marrow. The leftover bones were then scrubbed and strung together as souvenirs for guests to take home.[2] While Kaprow and Matta-Clark underscored the symbolic act of cooking and food in their work, Rirkrit Tiravanija's *Pad Thai* (1992) emphasized the tradition of sharing food with others as a means of building and identifying with a community. Tiravanija, who grew up in Thailand watching his grandmother cook in her restaurant, made and served the eponymous dish within a pristine museum or gallery setting, challenging ideas of what constitutes art. The performance and the resulting food created a dynamic relationship between the audience and the artist, questioning notions of power, ownership, and authorship.

Artists Sita Kuratomi Bhaumik and Mary Parisi engage both historic traditions—the performance of the self in the family kitchen and the performative act of cooking as art or the use of food as a medium in art. In Bhaumik's *To Curry Favor* (2011), the viewer is hit with a waft of curry-scented air before even entering the gallery. Once inside, smell joins sight as the viewer is drawn into the installation. Set against a striking array of plates and objects, some with curry roux underneath their gold candy-wrapper covers, the installation recalls the parlors of nineteenth-century homes where *horror vacuui* reigned as a decorating mantra. Here, Bhaumik connects to the tradition of performance by using food as a medium, but the work also draws from her multicultural background. Much like the complex mix of spices that constitute curry, the work touches on issues of race, class, culture, and immigration. Bottled and labeled "curry" by the British, who sought to recreate the flavors they tasted during their colonization of India, the spice blend eventually made its way to Japan via British naval ships. Bhaumik uses curry as a proclamation of where she is from and who she is, its journey a map of her own family ancestry.

By focusing on the strikingly beautiful yet sometimes alienating qualities of food, Parisi disrupts our passive relationship to what we consume and the role it plays in shaping our memories. Stemming from her recollection of making soup with her father as a young girl, Parisi's series *Food Pictures* depicts the unease of "meeting your meat"—the moment when "food" is reconciled as "animal." She remembers looking forward to the weekly ritual of making soup and the moment when this simple comfort was made more complicated when she witnessed her father adding chicken feet to the broth. The sight horrified Parisi, who until then had thought of meat as coming from the supermarket in neatly wrapped, anonymous packages. She encapsulates this moment in the photograph *Unnamed Chicken* (2007). In *Unnamed*, a whole roasting chicken is portrayed as a victim drowning in its own broth, the camera's lens acting as the "ice" trapping it under water. By "performing" a version of making soup with her father, Parisi reenacts the activity, connecting to and intensifying the memory by physical action. In humanizing the animal, she forces viewers to empathize with their dinner and to consider parallels between the animal world and the human world.

Economist Paul Roberts states, "Food itself is almost the physical embodiment of emotional and social forces: the object of our strongest desire; the basis of our oldest memories and earliest relationships."[3] These formative experiences shape us in conspicuous and imperceptible ways, binding us inextricably to our history. If butter and flour simmered together in a pan makes many of our best loved recipes possible, then identity can be understood as a complex "roux" of behaviors, history, aesthetics, and aspirations performed daily. As a recipe handed down through generations and customized to taste year after year, identity is both foundational and fluctuating, and we are equally a consequence and a celebration of the ingredients.

[1] Barbara Kirshenblatt-Gimblett, "Playing to the Senses: Food as a Performance Medium," *Performance Research* 4.1 (1999): 1-30.
[2] Randy Kennedy, "When Meals Played the Muse," *New York Times* (2007): 1.
[3] Paul Roberts, "The New Food Anxiety," *Psychology Today* 31 (1998): 30.

TURNING TABLES

Nicole J. Caruth

In the early 1970s, the California-based photographer Bill Owens began to document the suburban boom in the San Francisco Bay Area. Every Saturday for a year he photographed suburban residents in and around their homes, posed in modern kitchens, barbequing in the backyard, seated around the dinner table, and hosting Tupperware parties; food figures prominently in these portraits. *Untitled (Joy of Cooking)* is possibly his most poignant image. It shows, rather simply, a kitchen pantry filled mostly with canned and packaged foodstuffs. At that time, such an abundance of artificial foods was a sign of prosperity, a sort of edible wealth that spoke to the material comforts of middle-class American life and the American Dream. Nowadays that same pantry might signify financial poverty, poor food education, obesity, malnutrition, and the threat of heart disease. The tables have certainly turned.

In the years since Owens's *Suburbia* series, Americans have only gotten further away from producing the foods they eat. You might be challenged to find an adolescent who knows the origins of the ketchup or pickles that adorn their fast-food burgers or even an adult who believes that a tomato or cucumber was ever part of the equation. It's no wonder, then, that health statistics are so grim: over a billion people—one seventh of the world's population—are considered overweight or obese. And another billion suffer from "hidden hunger," the lack of essential vitamins and nutrients in their diets.[1] But there's good news: more people than ever before are taking an interest in what they eat and where it comes from. A nearly palpable spirit of celebration around food and cooking marks our present moment (just look at the plethora of television shows, magazines, and websites dedicated to the subject), as do serious debates about how we can better cultivate and consume foods for healthier futures (it's not for nothing that farmers, organic agriculture, and all things "green" are in vogue). *Acquired Taste* takes stock of what's happening in food today, giving us a sense of where we are and where we might be going.

Jennifer Rubell's installation, *Old Fashioned,* elevates cheap fast food—the quintessence of our national culture—to edible high art. Each of nearly 1,500 nails in the wall is ornamented with an "old-fashioned" variety of Dunkin Donut.[2] Viewers are invited to partake of the installation. First shown at Art Basel Miami Beach, the piece might be taken as a symbol of excess in the art world—and also beyond. Sprawling 60 feet across, 8 feet high, and repeatedly restocked as doughnuts run low, *Old Fashioned* calls to mind a sense of infinite availability and the proliferation of Dunkin Donuts itself; the franchise seems to appear at virtually every city corner and highway rest stop across the United States. So goes the motto "America runs on Dunkins." At the same time, the installation sometimes bears resemblance to an LED billboard; as doughnuts are removed from the grid, it looks as if a message might be spelled out on the wall, an optical effect that evokes modern technology's role in food advertisement and daily marketing to adults and children.

Food is not just hypervisible in ads and entertainment media today, it is also hyperreal. Pamela Johnson's large-scale paintings of all-American junk food walk the line between harmless "food porn" (a phenomenon of current popular culture) and dangerous fetishization. Hostess Cupcakes, M & M's, Top Ramen, Kool-Aid, and PB&J on Wonder Bread rendered against dark backgrounds appear ominous. They seem to warn us against instant gratification. Johnson's aesthetic treatment of food harks back to the Pop artist Claes Oldenburg, who sculpted burgers, cake, and ice cream cones at extreme and sometimes scatological proportions, suggesting both an embrace of the everyday object as art and distaste for the excessive. Again, glut has not been without consequence. How can we look upon a giant cupcake or a great wall of doughnuts and not think about rising rates of food-related illnesses, not to mention the ecological effects of mass production and consumption?

While food is cheaper and more readily available than it used to be, by now it's obvious that we've paid for it in other ways. Timothy Berg and Rebekah Myers explore the relationship between human appetites and the natural world with their giant Popsicle sculpture *Here Today, Gone Tomorrow.* The title is as telling as their materials. Fiberglass and lacquer read as the stuff of industrial plants and car factories. That a whole Popsicle is juxtaposed with its two leftover color-stained sticks suggests an antagonism between the pleasures of consumption and a degrading environmental resource. The contrast of sticks might also represent the shift from a booming car industry to a troubling one. In the U.S., four out of every ten bushels of corn are grown to fuel motor vehicles.[3] With cars consuming calories and people consuming fuel, we are functioning on a system that is no more sustainable environmentally than it is socially. Enter artists like Greg Stewart and Tattfoo Tan who are growing crops, proposing new farming models, and engaging new communities in the process.

Stewart's *Movable Gardens* consist of edible fruit and vegetable trees planted in mobile carts (complete with 5-gallon water tanks, or buckets, for maintenance) that move from one neighborhood to another before they eventually migrate back to the space of the exhibition. They are as much about disseminating urban agriculture as they are about spreading public art to new environments. Though Stewart's *Movable Gardens* may or may not be a feasible solution for feeding a community, they at least get us thinking about the potential future of food. In the United States, where food is plentiful, it can be hard to imagine that the amount of land available to cultivate crops would ever be scarce. But, already, food shortages and increasing prices for basic foods are causing riots in various parts of the world. The small farm mobility that Stewart proposes with his artwork, then, could end up being essential to human survival.

Even in our globalized society, local food discourses can be entangled with fallacious notions of "authentic" food products and experiences. Like Stewart, Sita Kuratomi Bhaumik's work with food is inspired by human migratory patterns, which are anything but absolute. Born in Los Angeles and of Bengali and Japanese-Colombian descent, Bhaumik has described her work as being born of the playful character Willy Wonka and the cultural theorist Edward Said.[4] Sugars and spices are her primary materials. *Hey, Sugar Sugar*, a welcome mat made of powdered sugar, conjures the idea that food is a gateway to different cultures. But Bhaumik's works in both curry and sugar, which overlap and intersect in paisley and lace-like patterns, suggest the problem with that mindset: while food and cooking can reveal idiosyncrasies of certain ethnicities, they will often also reveal how they intersect with other cultures. Upon entering the gallery, the viewer is not only confronted with various aromas but also the histories of trade, war, and miscegenation that sugar and spices typically embody, histories that are constantly changing and in flux.

In Stephen Shanabrook's hands, food is a way to intimately connect, though not with cultures, communities, or even the zeitgeist, but with the deceased. With *Dexter*-like humor, he casts dark chocolate molds from the fatal wounds of anonymous dead people in morgues. Shotgun holes in the face, broken fingers, and other injured body parts are exhibited like See's Candies. Viewers are likely conflicted: you want to look but you don't want to. You don't want to desire these chocolates but you just might. Shanabrook's recent chocolate sculptures of postdetonation suicide bombers appear to make light of recent war casualties. But the bitter irony of his work is how banal foods, like chocolate, might actually provide comfort in times of tragedy.

Artists in *Acquired Taste* remind us of what artist's do best: show us new ways of looking at the everyday world around us. In so doing, they offer up new ideas that might push us forward ever so slightly as a culture or at least show us, as Owens did with *Untitled (Joy of Cooking)*, how the calories we consume can also consume us.

[1] Prince Charles of Wales, Keynote Address, Future of Food Conference, Georgetown University, Washington D.C., 4 May 2011.

[2] Though discussed here, Rubell's installation *Old Fashioned* was not included in *Acquired Taste*. A new work by the artist was decided on after this catalogue essay had been written.

[3] Prince Charles of Wales, Keynote Address, Future of Food Conference, 4 May 2011.

[4] Victoria Gannon, "Bedfellows: Hungry in San Francisco Part 2," *Art:21 blog*, 7 June 2011. See http://blog.art21.org/?s=Victoria+Gannon

Contemporary Confections is the blog of Nicole J. Caruth, a writer and curator of contemporary art who has a serious sweet tooth.

Caruth's articles on food and art have appeared in ARTnews, C Magazine, *and* Gastronomica. *She also writes a monthly column on the subject for the Art21 blog. Her writing will be featured in the forthcoming publication:* Vitamin Green, *a Phaidon Press book on sustainable architecture and green design. Caruth's recent curatorial projects include* With Food in Mind *at the Center for Book Arts in New York.*

A native of the California Bay Area, Caruth received her Bachelor's degree from San Francisco State University, where she studied art history with Dr. Judith Bettelheim and Dr. Whitney Chadwick. She earned her Master's degree from the Center for Curatorial Studies at Bard College.

GLAZED IMAGES

Megan Fizell

As a species, we humans are predisposed to seek out sugar to supplement our diet. "Sweet tooth" and "sugar rush" are colloquial phrases used to describe our bodies' cravings for and reaction to the substance. In nature, sugar is found in the simple form of fructose produced within the flesh of ripe fruits. According to food activist Michael Pollan, fructose is "a rare and precious thing, typically encountered seasonally…when it comes packaged in a whole food, full of fibre which slows its absorption and valuable micronutrients."[1] In the shape of fruit, sugar has riddled the paintings of the Western tradition dating back to the Northern Renaissance;[2] however, in more contemporary works it is ominously absent. How closely does what we, as a culture, depict in art mirror what we consume?

The rise of the pop art movement saw the birth of confectionary imagery used to highlight consumption and excess. In the early 1960s, Wayne Thiebaud painted cakes in balanced and simplified compositions suggesting the counter displays of cafeterias and delicatessens. He cleverly used a thick application of paint to mimic the look and texture of frosting, underlining the idea of "object transference" for works in which the paint literally assumes the appearance of the element it is depicting. During this movement, Claes Oldenburg made his 1962 sculpture *Floor Cake*, a soft sculpture made of canvas and filled with foam rubber and cardboard boxes. The swelling structure of the cake echoed the abundance found in Thiebaud's paintings. It was at this time that the American diet began to change as well. Not only were cakes and pastries appearing on canvases, they were conveniently prepackaged en masse under the banners of the Hostess and Little Debbie companies, enabling Americans to readily consume at will.

The presence of processed sugar prevails in the recent work by contemporary artists selected for *Acquired Taste: Food and the Art of Consumption*. Sita Kuratomi Bhaumik welcomes gallery visitors with a doormat made of powdered sugar, while Pamela Johnson depicts partially consumed junk food in paintings such as *Ice Cream* of 2010, and Dustin Wayne Harris offers images of sticky confections in digital photographs such as *Chloe II* of 2009. The oversize build of the popsicles in *Here Today, Gone Tomorrow* by MyersBerg Studios is a less-than-subtle nod to Oldenburg's work in that it presents the audience with a before-and-after illustration of consumption.

Considering the trend of contemporary artists to focus their efforts on processed sugar, it is important to note that 40% of the artists in *Acquired Taste* either use or portray junk food in their work. Our predisposition to seek out the sweet stuff speaks to the pervasiveness of sugar in the visual arts. According to data from the U.S. Department of Agriculture, the average American consumes around 2,673 calories per day with 1,100 of them in the form of fat and sugar. These statistics inadvertently correlate; 40% of the works in the exhibition depict sugar, while 41% of the calories from the daily American diet are consumed as fat and sugar.[3] If the spectrum of dishes and delicacies presented in *Acquired Taste* is anything to go by, we really do depict the foods we love to eat.

[1] Michael Pollan, *In Defense of Food: An Eater's Manifesto* (New York: Penguin, 2008): 112
[2] Norbert Schneider, *Still Life Painting in the Early Modern Period* (Cologne: Taschen, 2003): 121.
[3] Tom Philpott, "The American Diet in One Chart, with Lots of Fats and Sugars," *Grist* 5, April 2011.
See http://www.grist.org/industrial-agriculture/2011-04-05-american-diet-one-chart-lots-of-fats-sugars

Megan Fizell is a Sydney-based art historian, writer and freelance photographer concerned with the representation of food in the visual arts. She holds a Master's degree in art history from Sotheby's Institute of Art in London and an MA in art business. She has worked as an associate at a number of art galleries and co-authored the book, Slow Burn – a century of Australian women artists.

Fizell's blog, Feasting on Art, has been featured in ARTnews Magazine, MiNDFOOD Magazine, Virgin Blue Voyeur Magazine, The Flint Journal, Wentworth Courier and on Bon Appetit, SBS Food, *Dolce & Gabbana's digital magazine* Swide, Design*Sponge, Eastside Radio, Glamour Magazine *website,* Fine Cooking, food52, GOOD, Culinate, Serious Eats, Photo of the Day, COLOURlovers, The World's Best Ever, Mental Floss, The Kitchn, MoCo Loco *and* 'Where the Wild Things Are' Official Blog.

Posts from Feasting on Art *are featured in the* 'Stir it Up' *section of the* Christian Science Monitor.

EXHIBITION

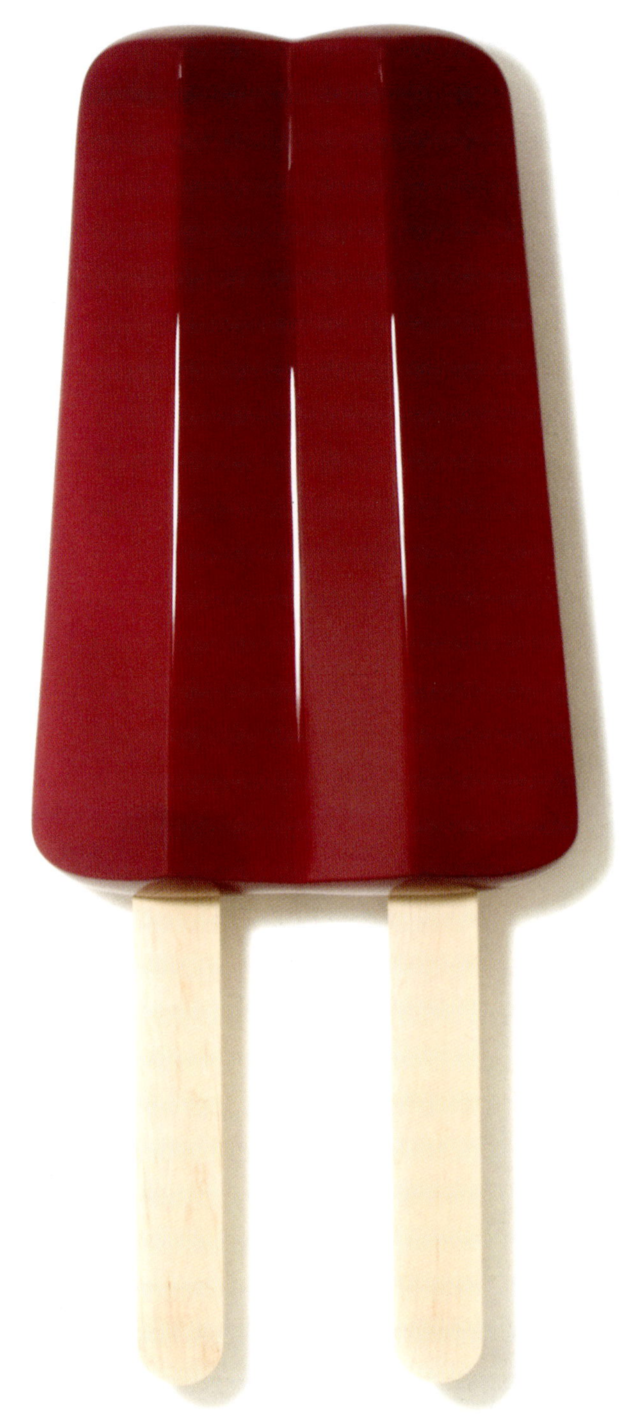

Here Today, Gone Tomorrow, 2011. Fiberglass urethane, paint, maple wood. 70 x 70 x 11 inches. Courtesy of the artists. (right) Installation, Begovich Gallery, CSU Fullerton.

TIM BERG & REBEKAH MYERS

The California-based *MeyersBerg Studios* duo creates sculptural work about humanity's impact on the environment. This piece gives a visual perspective on our overconsumption and contribution to the effects of global warming.

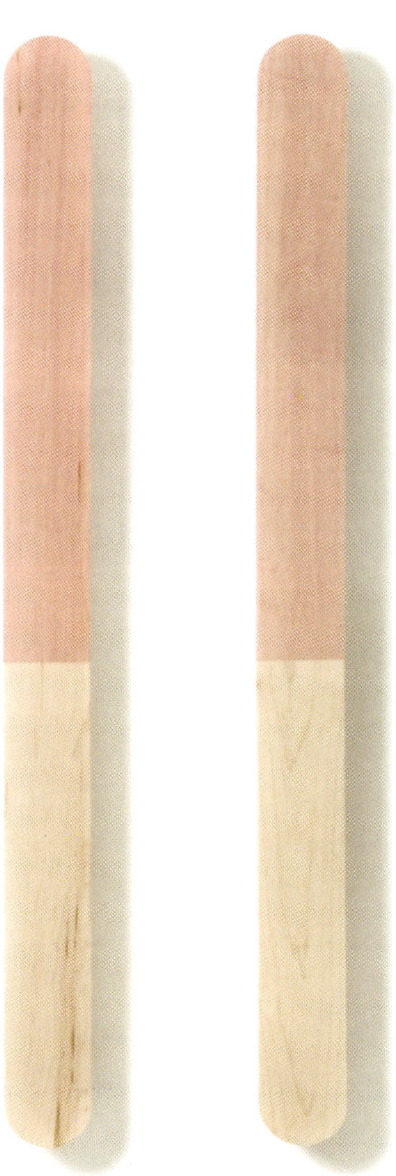

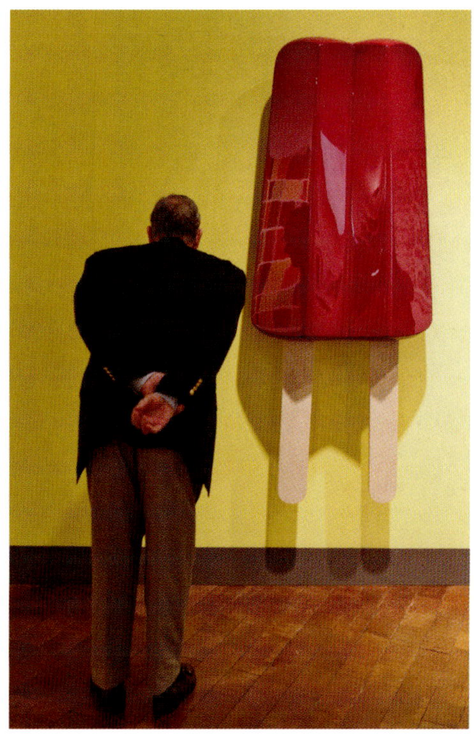

SITA KURATOMI BHAUMIK

To Curry Favor recalls a classic parlor space, only here the wallpaper is flocked with curry instead of velvet, and curry-scented plates covered in chocolate wrappers have replaced grandmother's good china. Bhaumik uses spice to allude to race, class and culture, challenging us to consider our own powerful memories associated with smell.

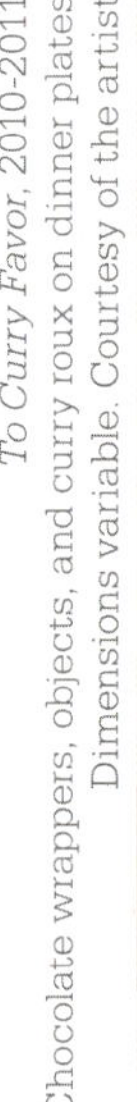

To Curry Favor (wallpaper), 2010-2011. Curry powder, spray adhesive. 3 x 20 feet. Courtesy of the artist.

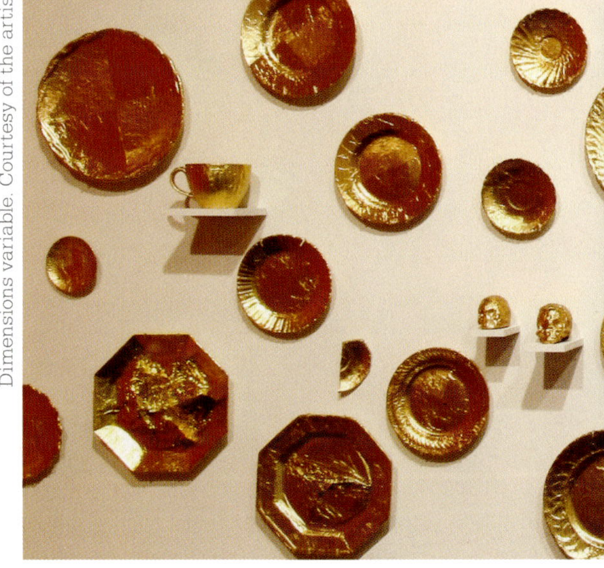

To Curry Favor, 2010-2011. Chocolate wrappers, objects, and curry roux on dinner plates. Dimensions variable. Courtesy of the artist.

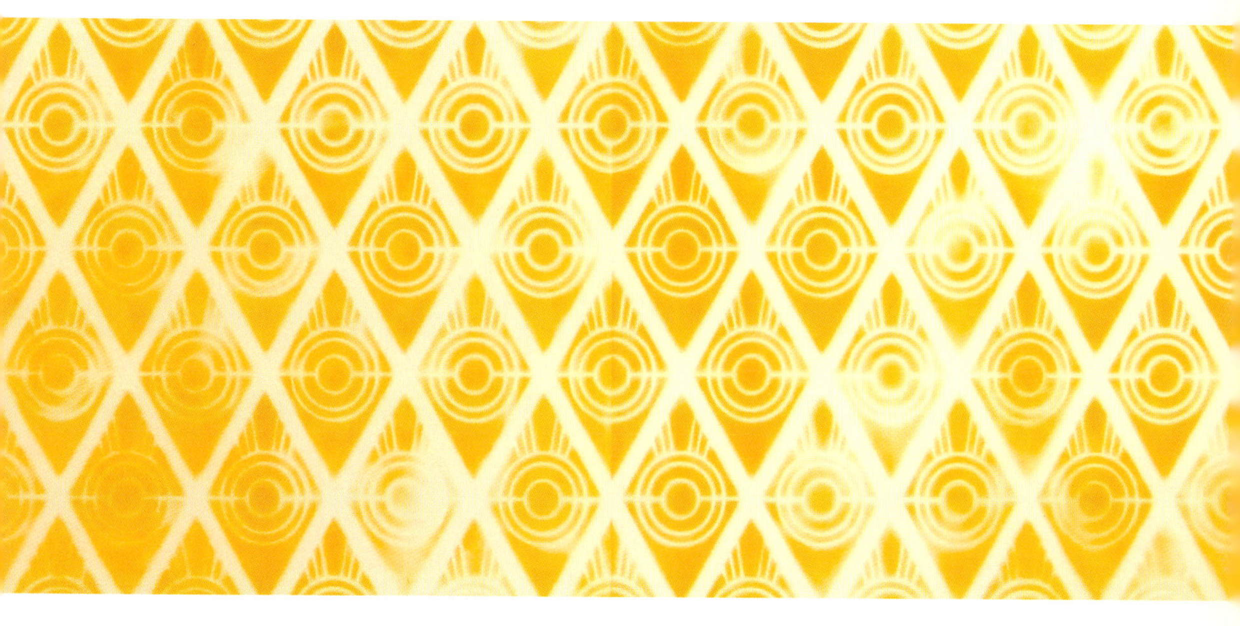

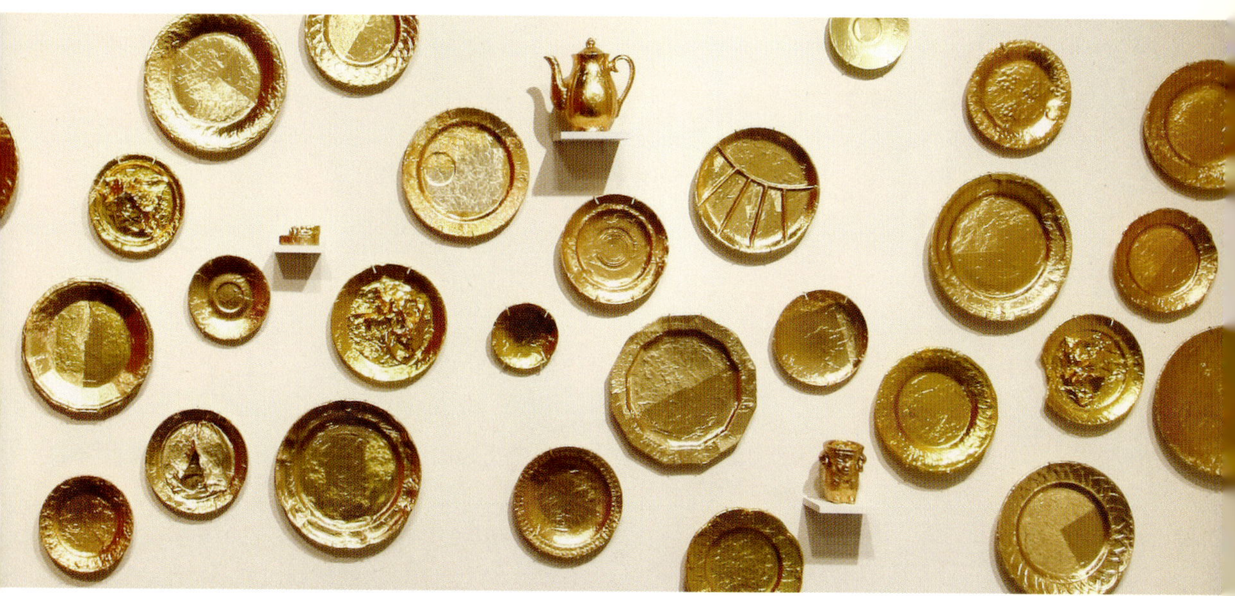

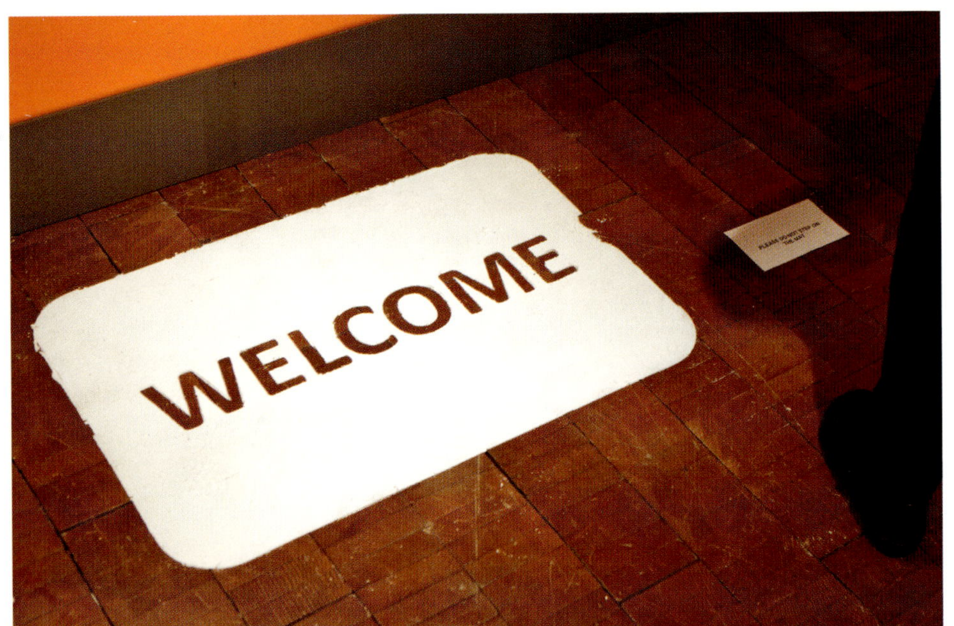

Hey, Sugar Sugar, 2010-2011. Powdered Sugar. Dimensions variable. Courtesy of the artist

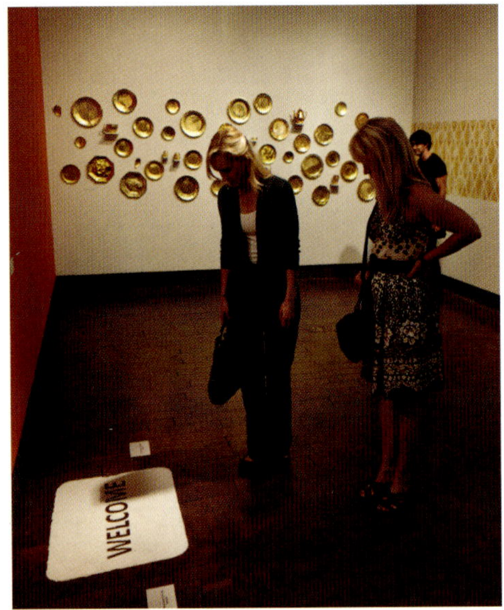

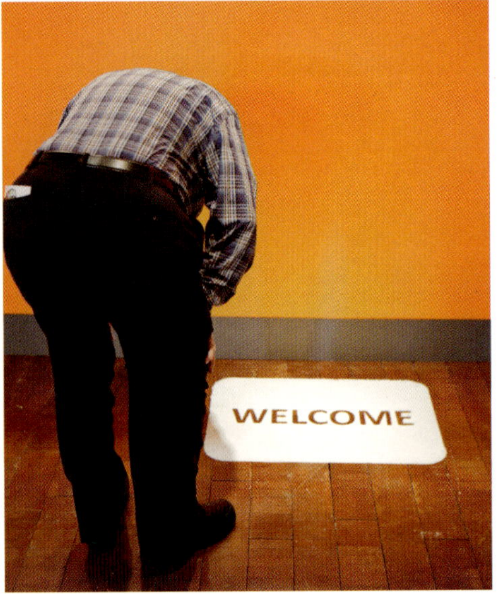

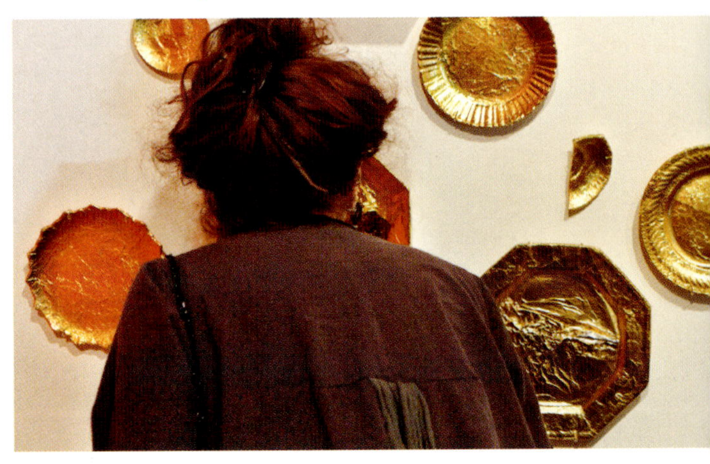

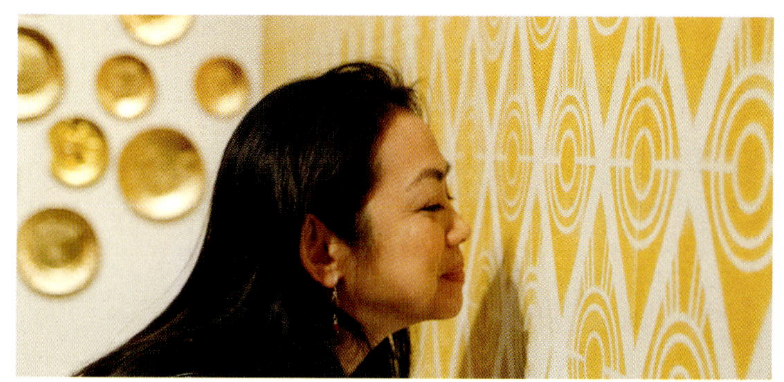

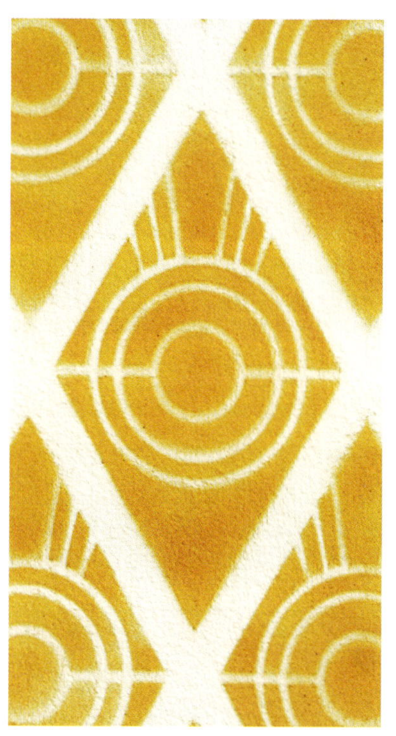

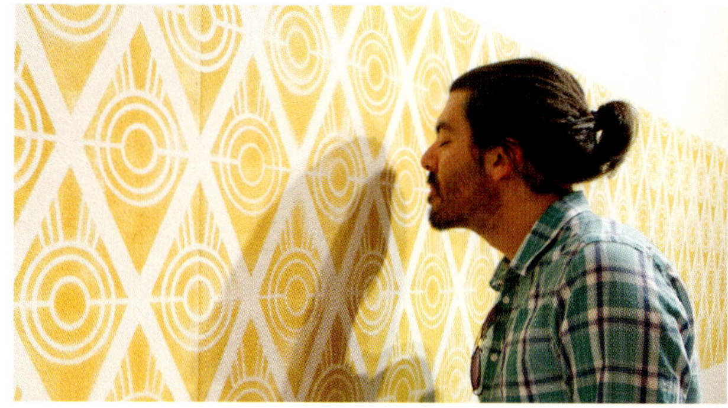

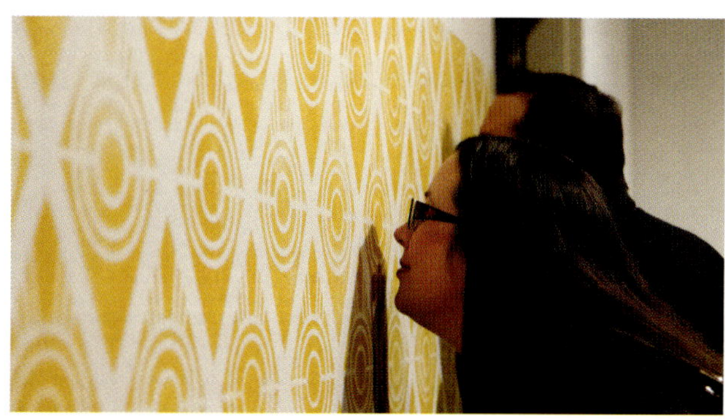

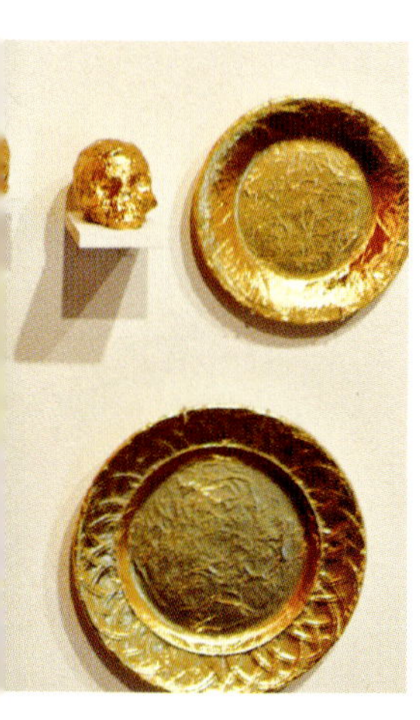

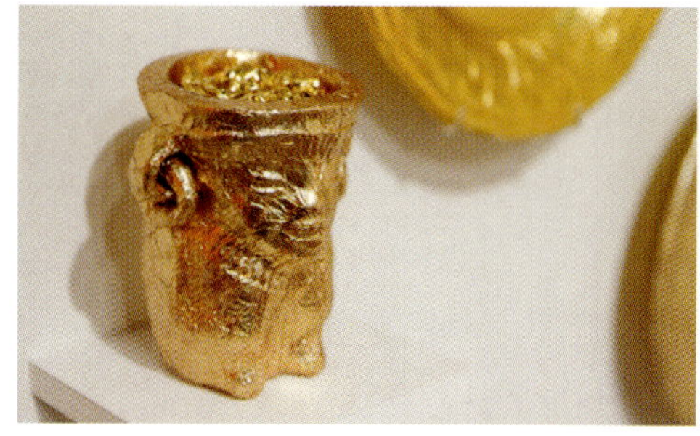

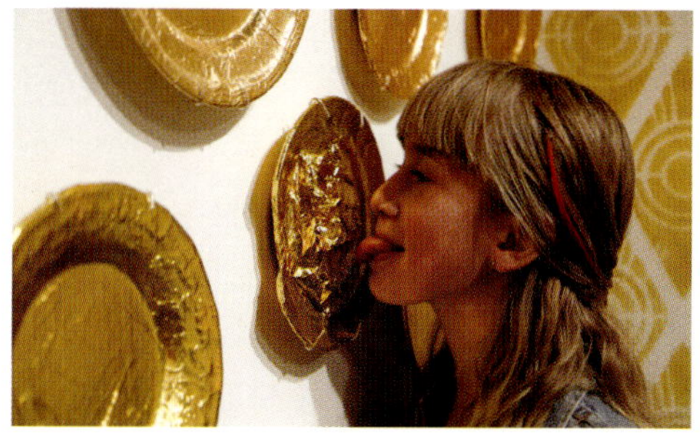

SHANNON HAYES FASELER

Inspired by the aftermath of Hurricane Katrina in New Orleans, Faseler's multimedia installation and paintings investigate the visual properties of mold growth in food and houses, and the unexpected beauty of degradation.

Installation assistants: Alyssa Cordova, Jessica Flores, Kevin Hill (video editor), Nahid Hosseini, Martin Lorigan, Patricia Reed, Heather Richards-Siddons, Rosemary Tesoro, Dee Dee

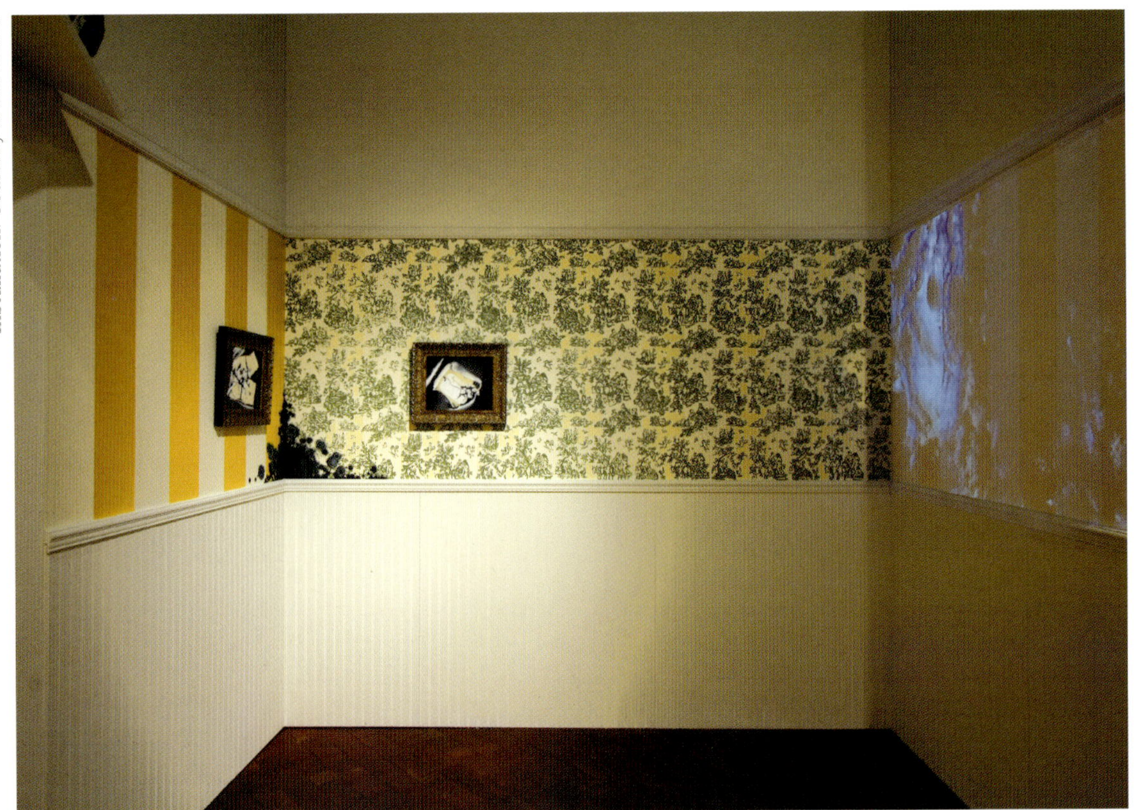

Aesthetics of Decay: Begovich, 2011. House paint, oil paint, video, wainscoting. Installation. Courtesy of the artist.

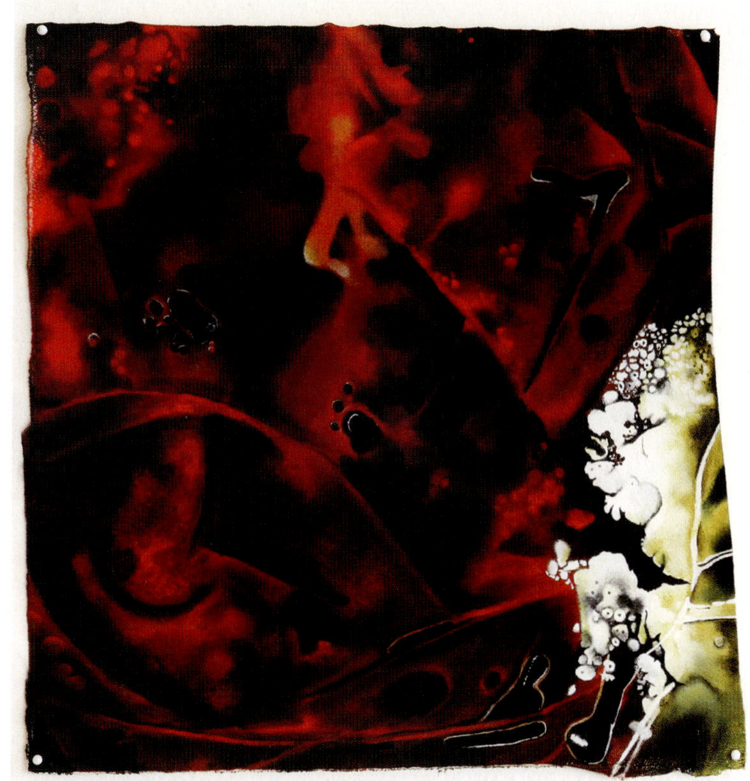

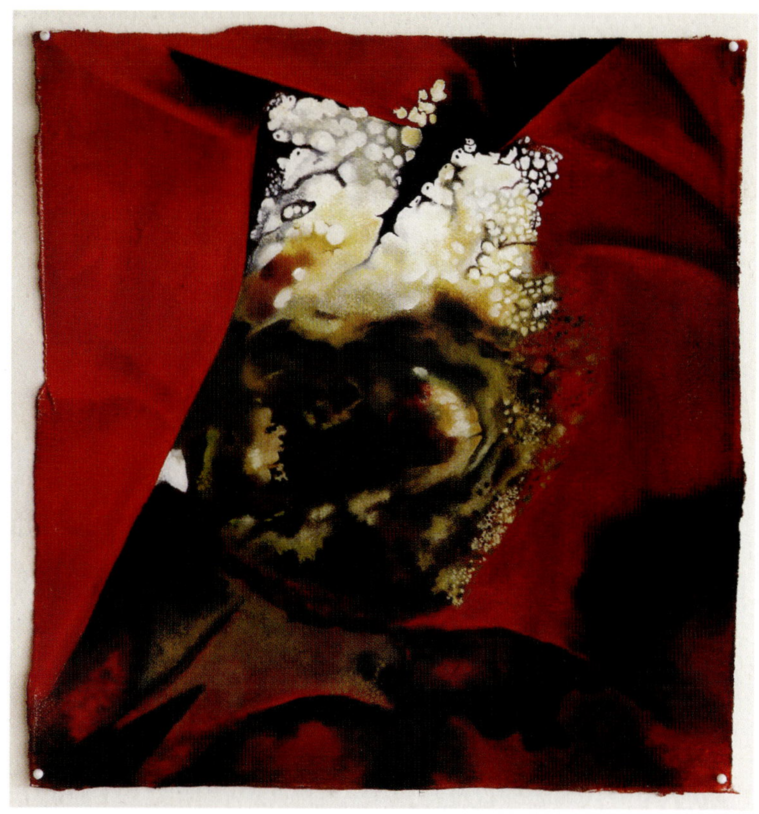

Tomato 1 & 2, 2009. Oil on paper. 12 x 12 inches. Courtesy of the artist.

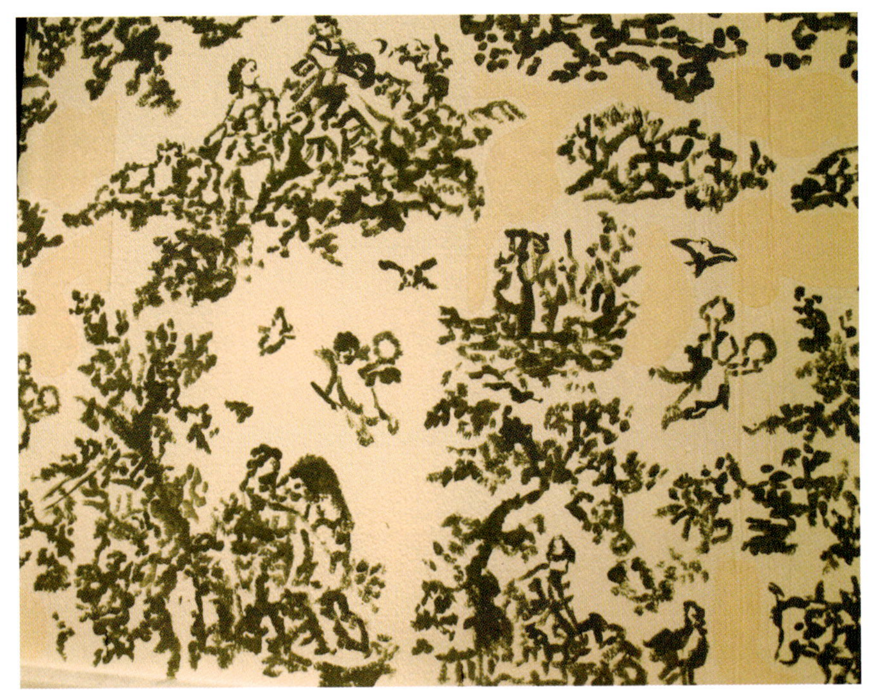

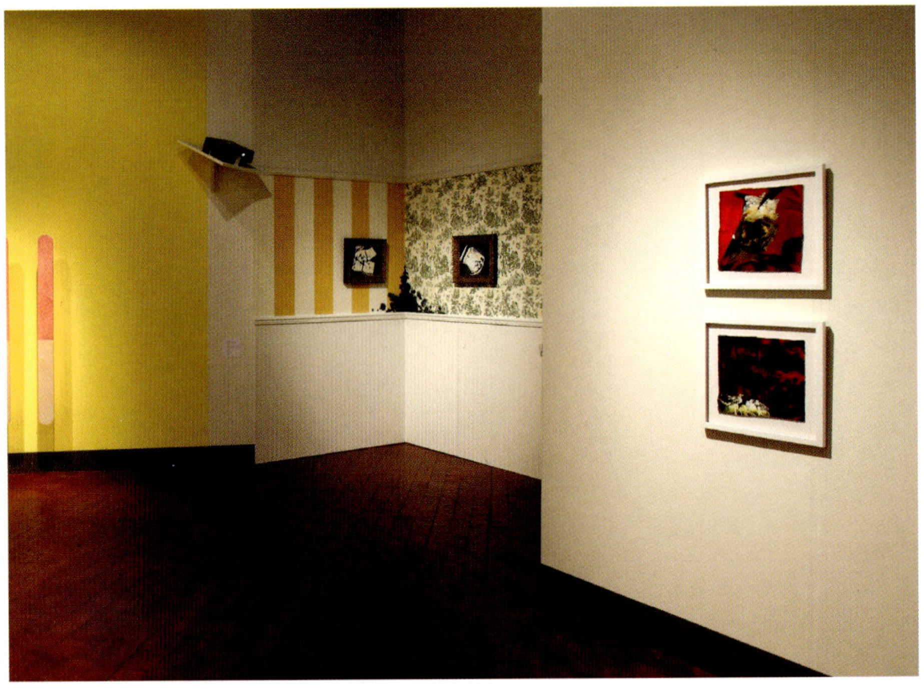

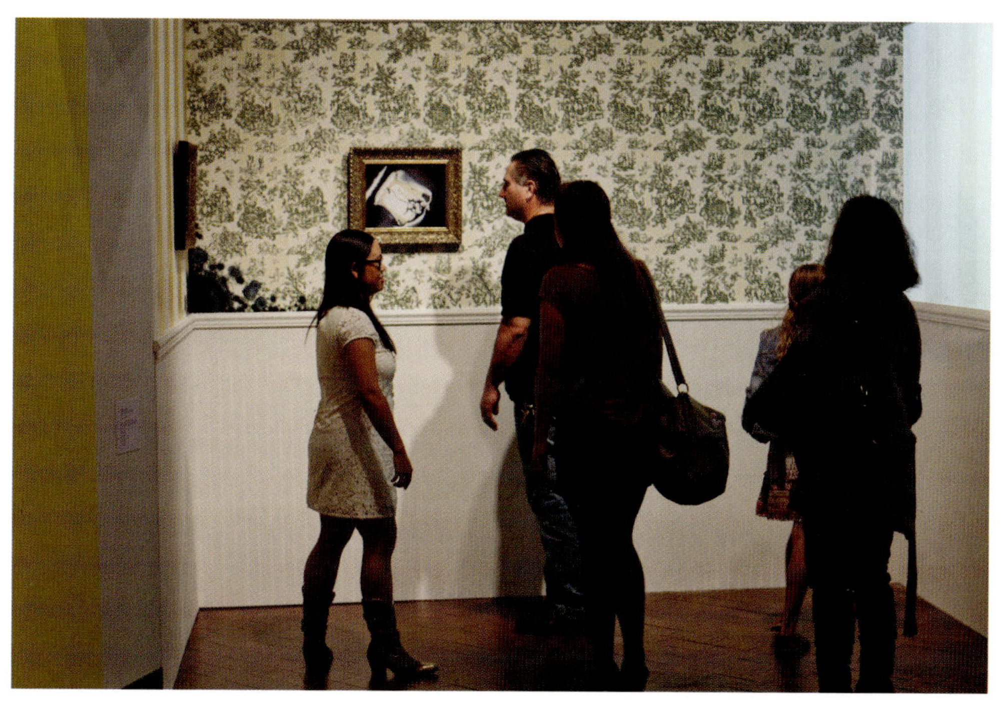

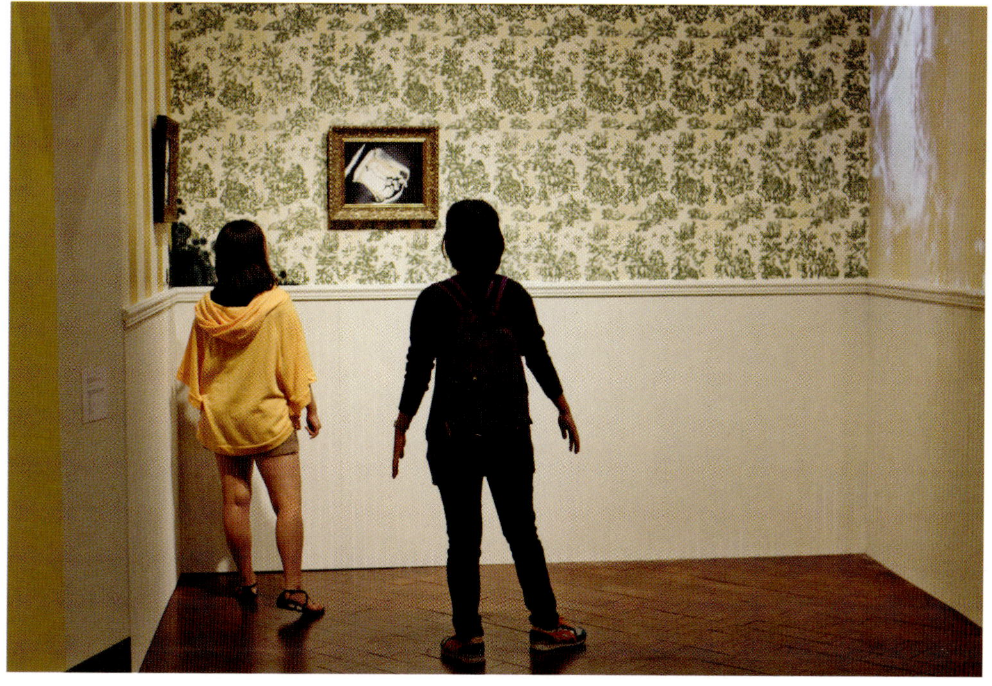

DUSTIN WAYNE HARRIS 

Harris's *Cake Mixx Series* turns the act of baking and decorating a cake into an exploration of interpersonal dynamics. Each cake depicted is named after the woman who baked it, all of whom knew Harris personally.

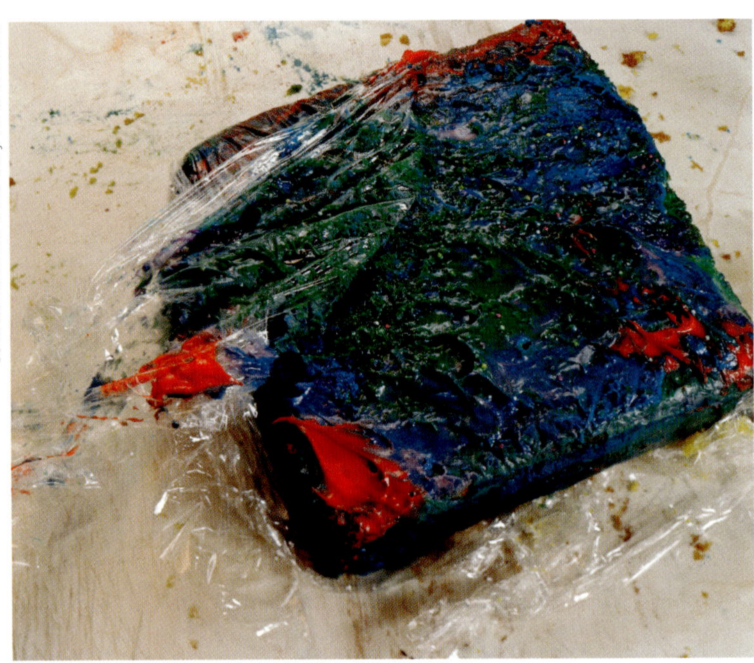

The Cake Mixx Series: Lindsey, 2009. Digital print. 16 x 20 inches. Courtesy of the artist.

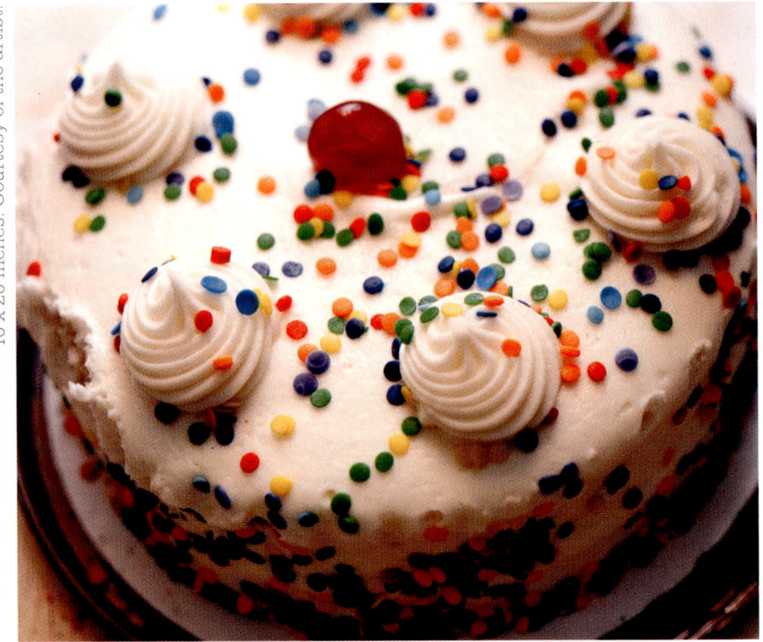

The Cake Mixx Series: Stephanie, 2009. Digital print. 16 x 20 inches. Courtesy of the artist.

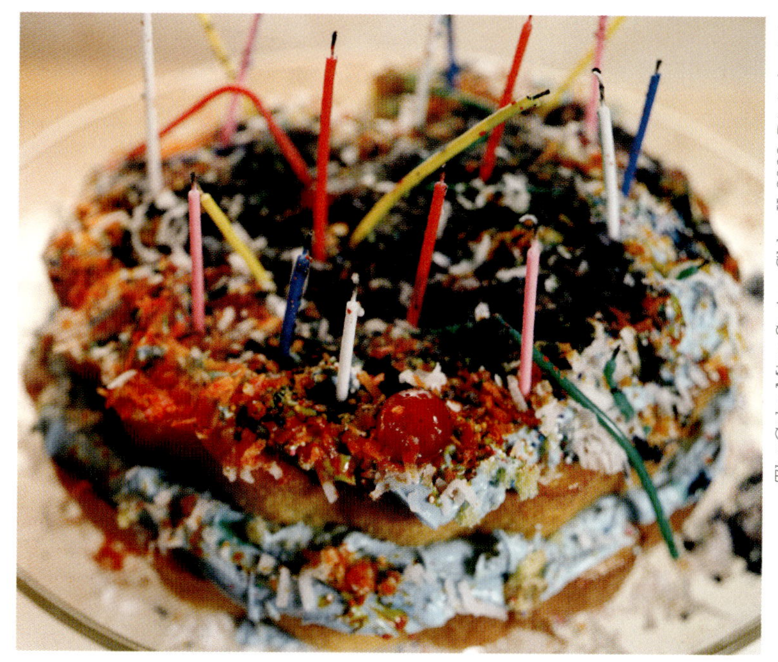

The Cake Mixx Series: Chloe II, 2009. Digital print.
16 x 20 inches. Courtesy of the artist.

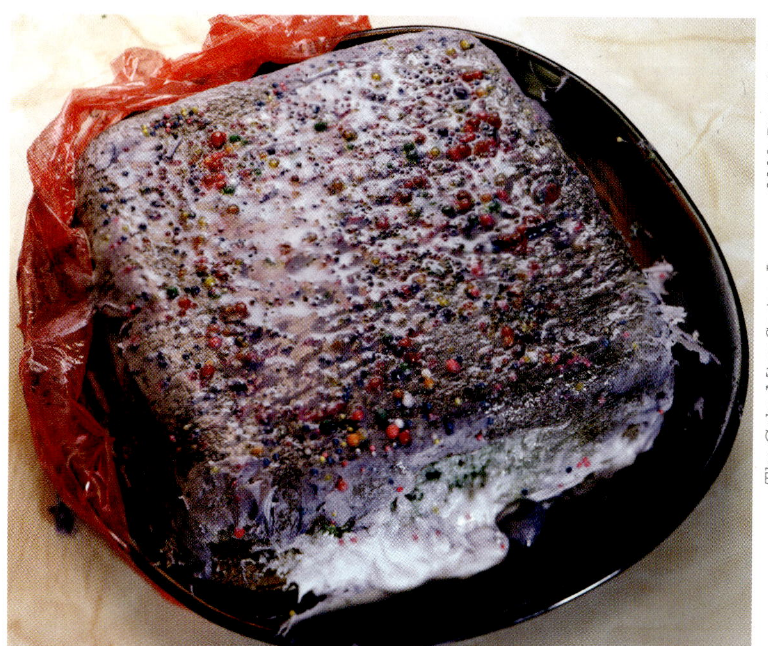

The Cake Mixx Series: Laryssa, 2009. Digital print.
16 x 20 inches. Courtesy of the artist.

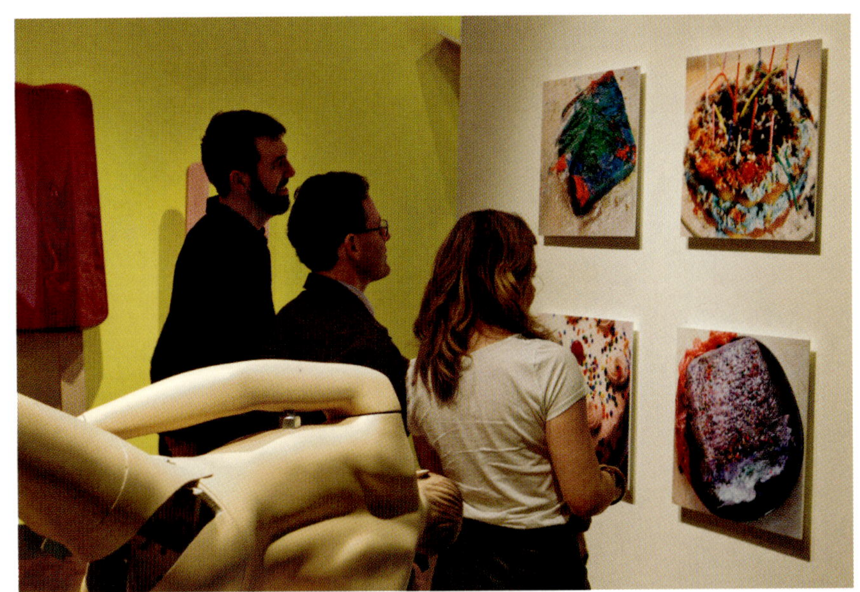

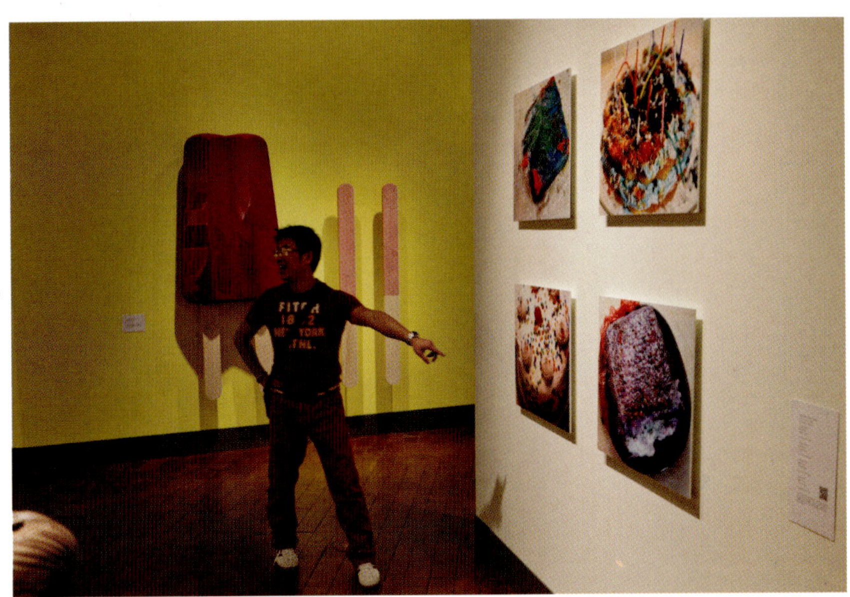

Installation, Begovich Gallery, CSU Fullerton.

PAMELA JOHNSON

Johnson's portraits of junk food reflect our Western cultural excesses. Bathed in stark light and set against a black void, the solitary wrappers and spilled food speak to our overindulgence and question the continued sustainability of our gluttony.

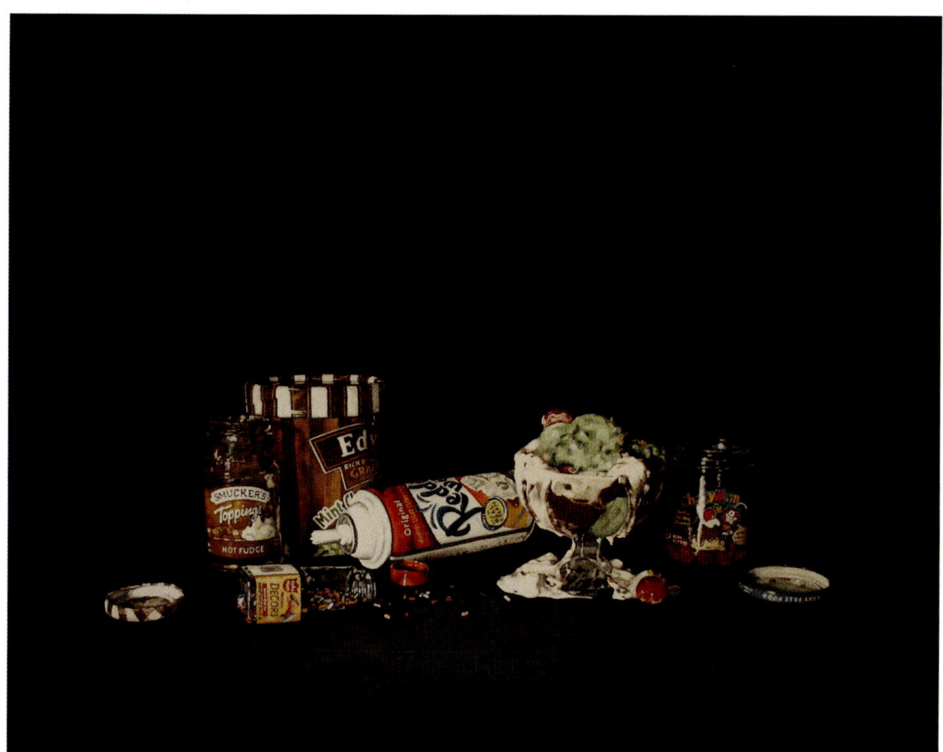

Ice Cream, 2010. Oil on canvas. 32 x 42 inches. Courtesy of Adler & Co. Gallery.

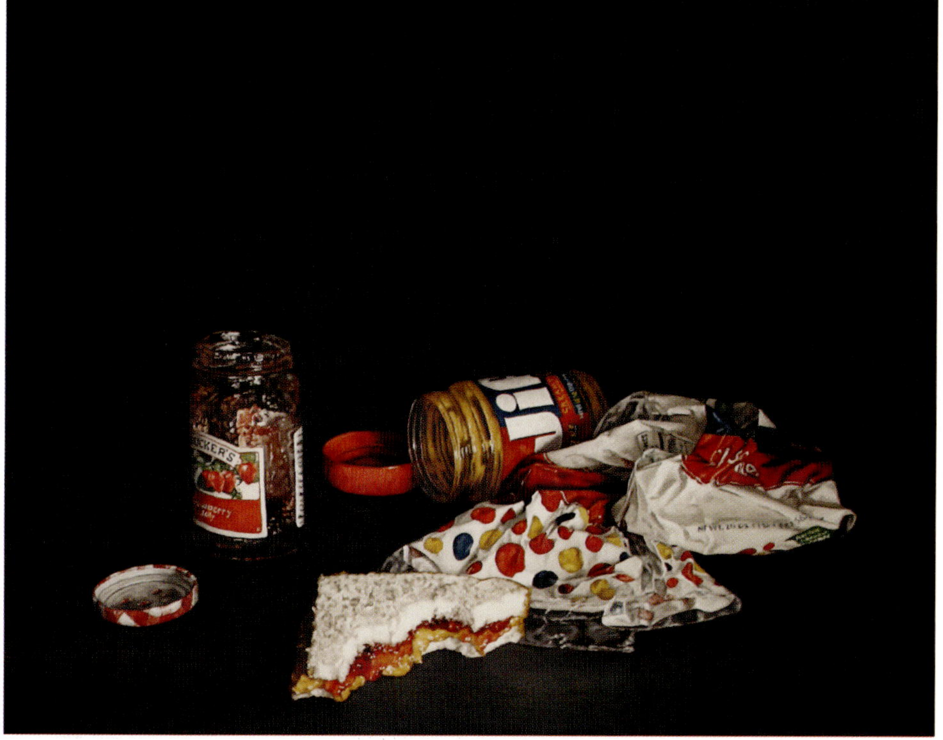

PB&J III, 2010. Oil on canvas. 32 x 42 inches. Courtesy of Adler & Co. Gallery.

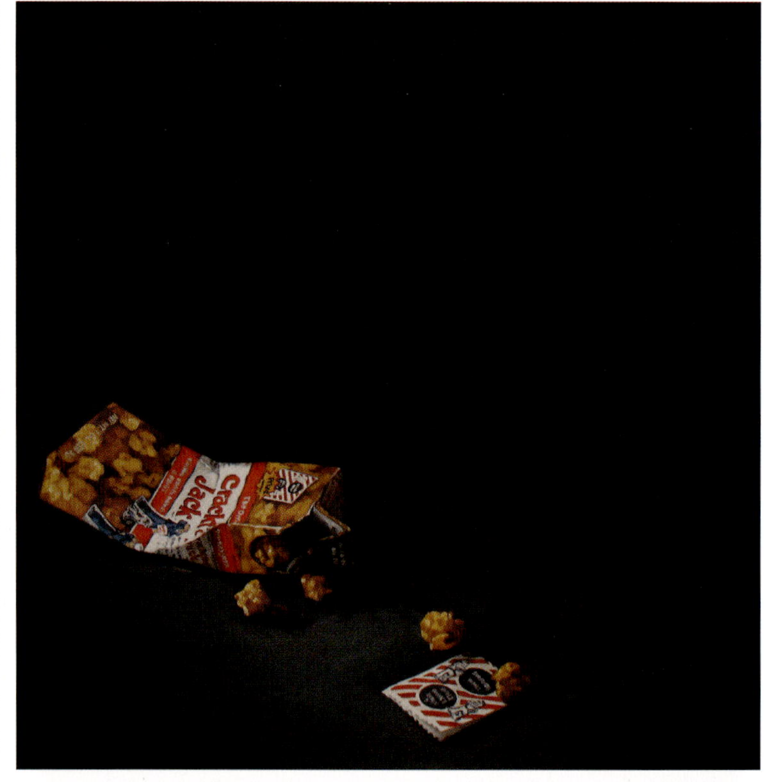

Cracker Jack, 2009. Oil on canvas. 20 x 20 inches. Courtesy of Adler & Co. Gallery.

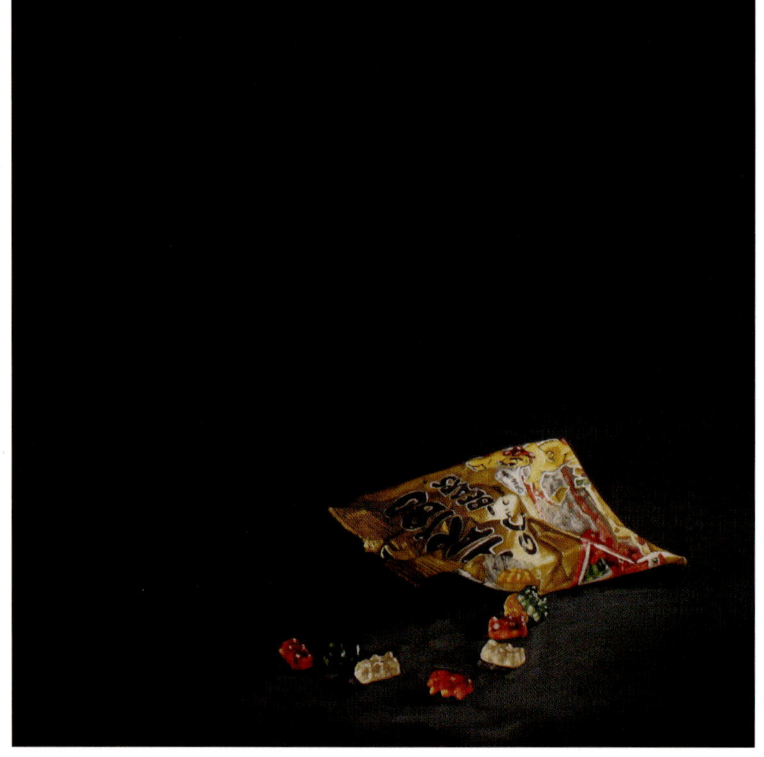

Gummi Bears, 2009. Oil on canvas. 20 x 20 inches. Courtesy of Adler & Co. Gallery.

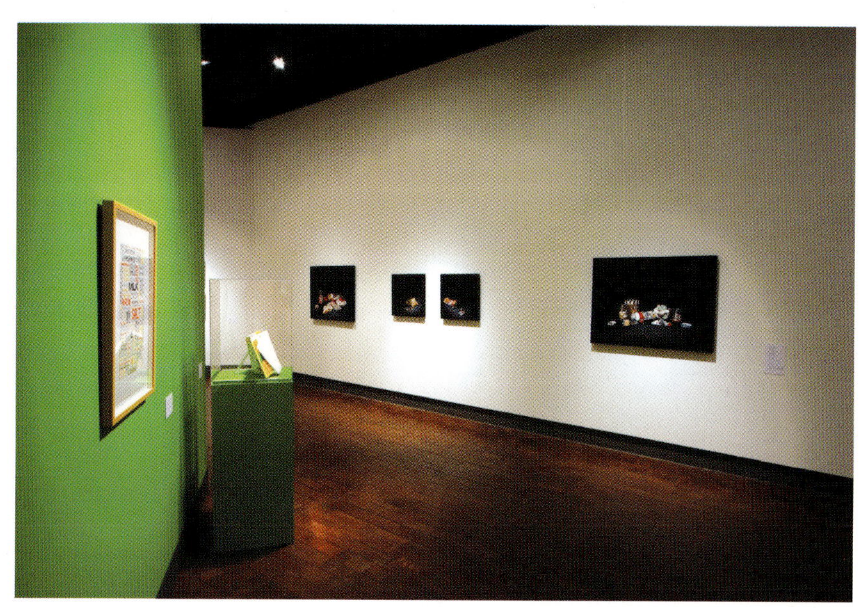

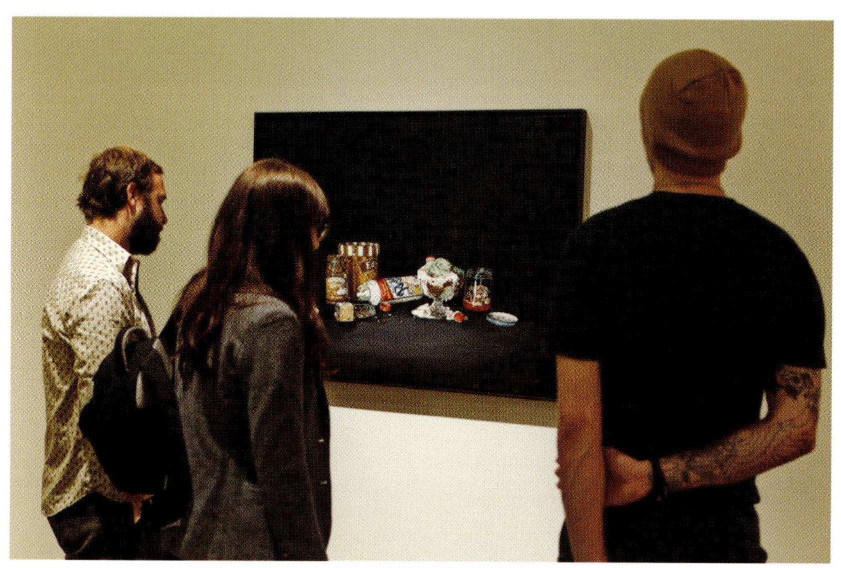

JENNIFER L. KNOX

Knox is a humorist and writer. This Mark Bittman cookbook was a wedding present for friends; she altered it with a black marker, glue and paper to include her own witty introduction.

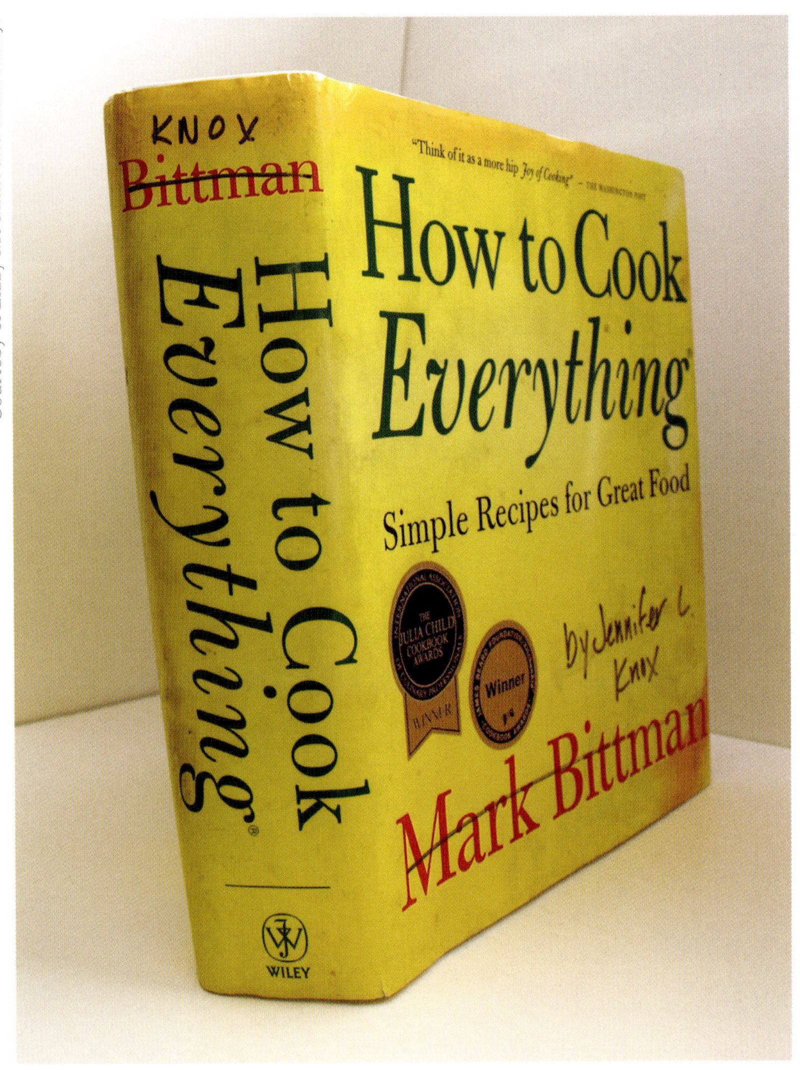

How to Cook Everything—Altered Book, 2010. Mixed media. 9.1 x 8.1 x 1.8 inchse. Courtesy of Lizzy McGlinn and Mark Reilly.

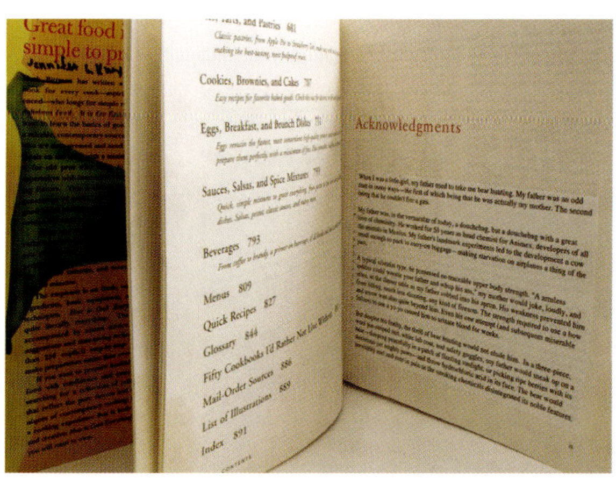

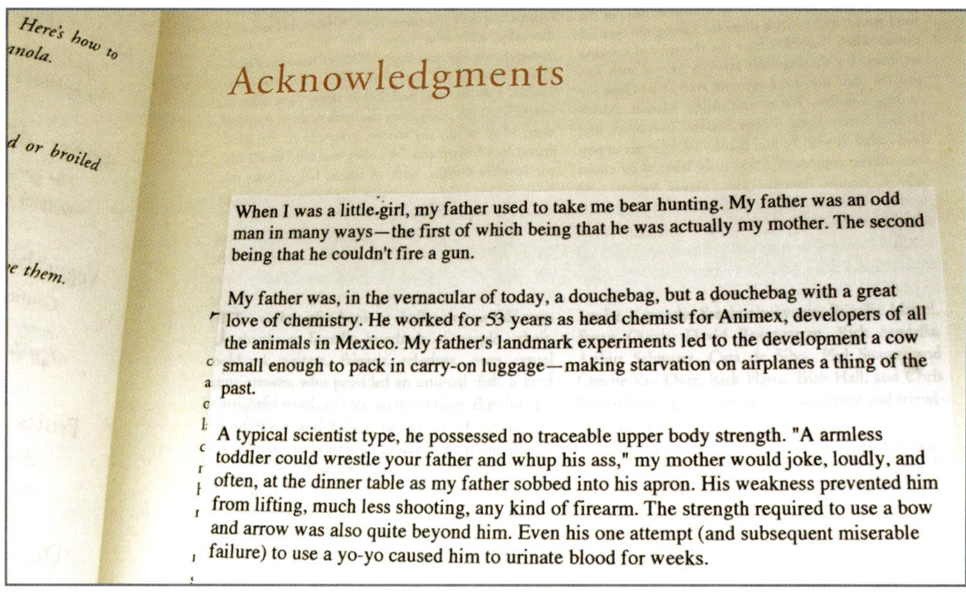

Acknowledgments

When I was a little girl, my father used to take me bear hunting. My father was an odd man in many ways—the first of which being that he was actually my mother. The second being that he couldn't fire a gun.

My father was, in the vernacular of today, a douchebag, but a douchebag with a great love of chemistry. He worked for 53 years as head chemist for Animex, developers of all the animals in Mexico. My father's landmark experiments led to the development a cow small enough to pack in carry-on luggage—making starvation on airplanes a thing of the past.

A typical scientist type, he possessed no traceable upper body strength. "A armless toddler could wrestle your father and whup his ass," my mother would joke, loudly, and often, at the dinner table as my father sobbed into his apron. His weakness prevented him from lifting, much less shooting, any kind of firearm. The strength required to use a bow and arrow was also quite beyond him. Even his one attempt (and subsequent miserable failure) to use a yo-yo caused him to urinate blood for weeks.

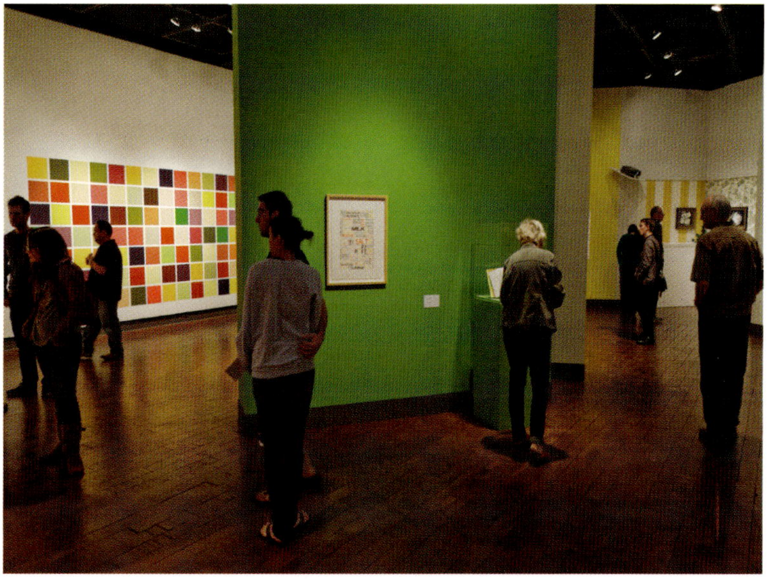

MARY PARISI 

Parisi's photographs focus on the beautiful yet alienating qualities of what we eat. As a child, Parisi watched her father drop chicken feet into homemade soup to flavor the broth, later making it impossible for her to regard animals as merely food.

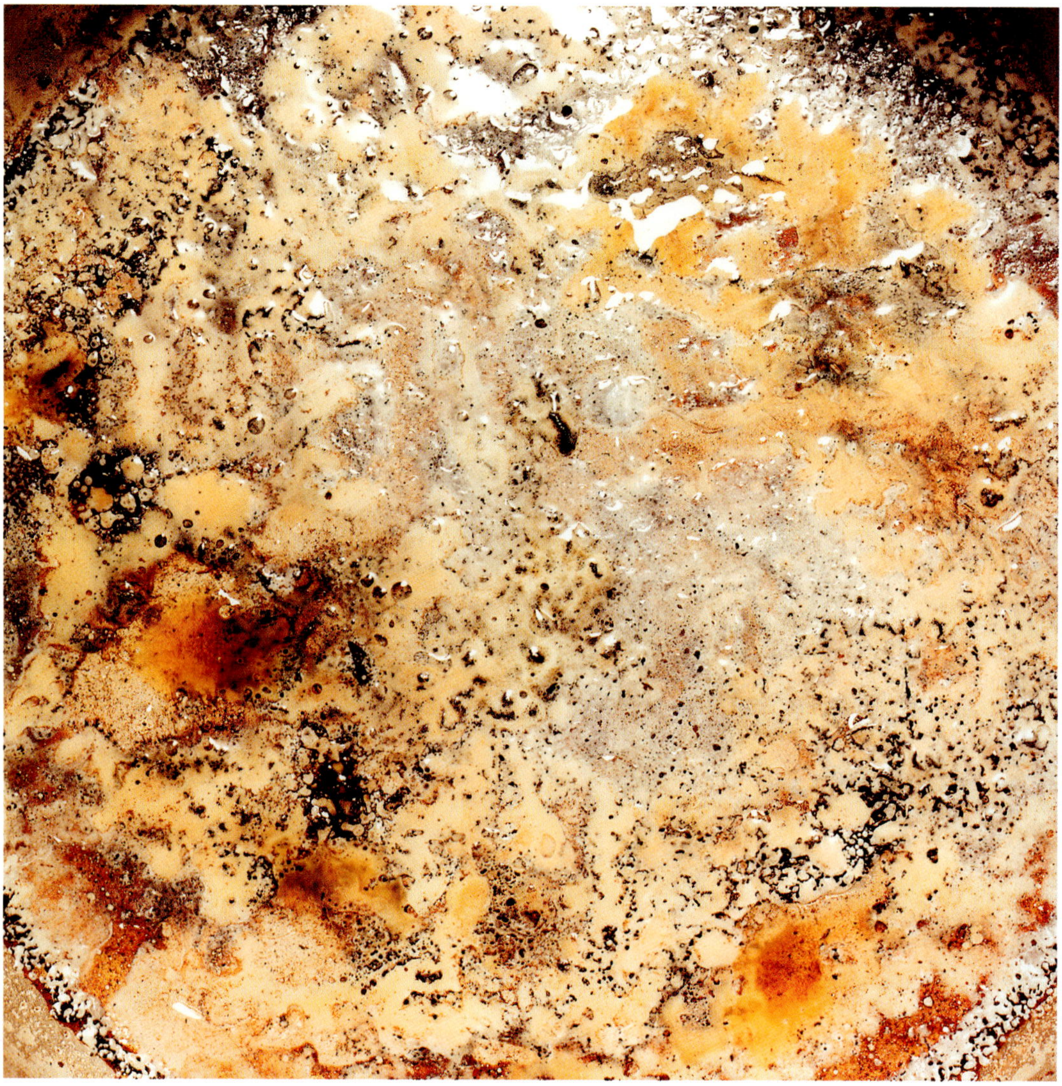

Burnt Pan, 2010. C-print. 30 x 30 inches. Courtesy of the artist.

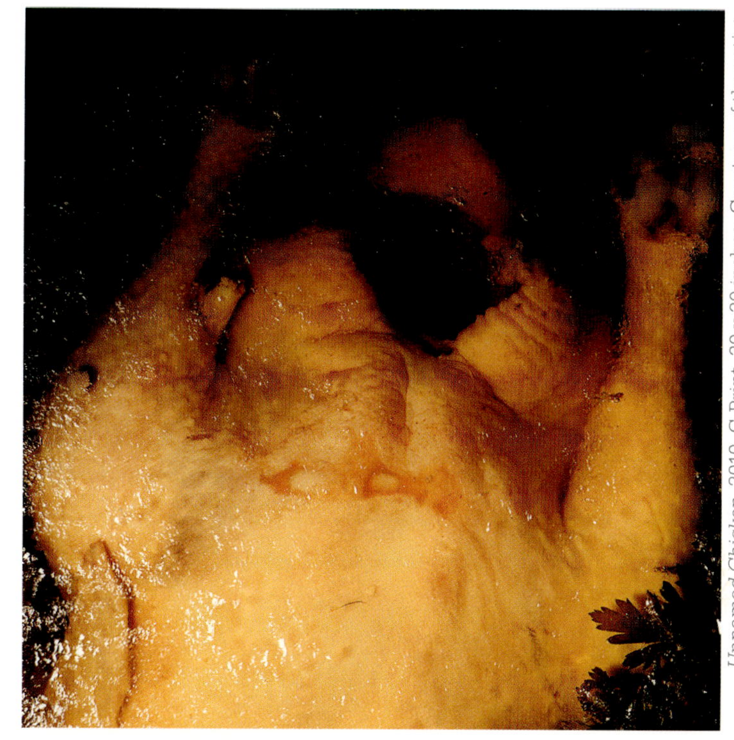

Unnamed Chicken, 2010. C-Print. 30 x 30 inches. Courtesy of the artist.

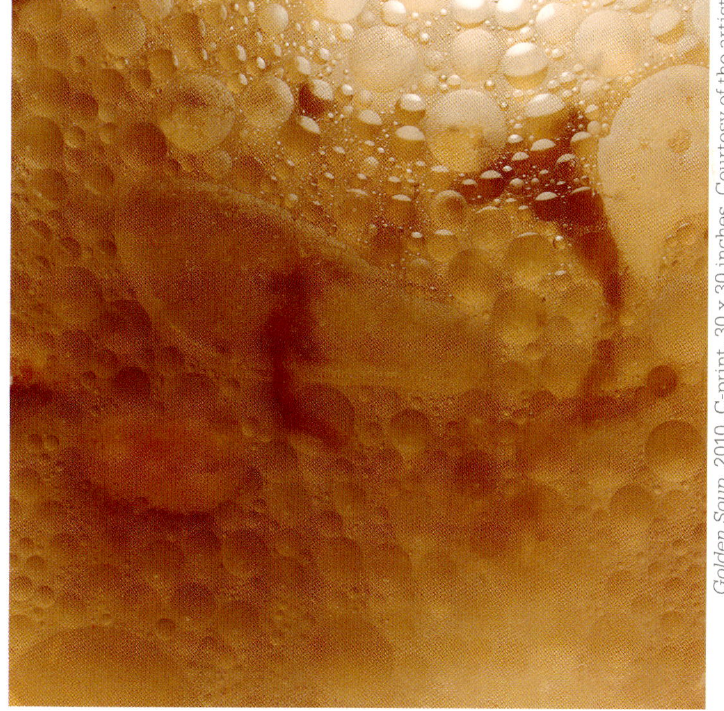

Golden Soup, 2010. C-print. 30 x 30 inches. Courtesy of the artist.

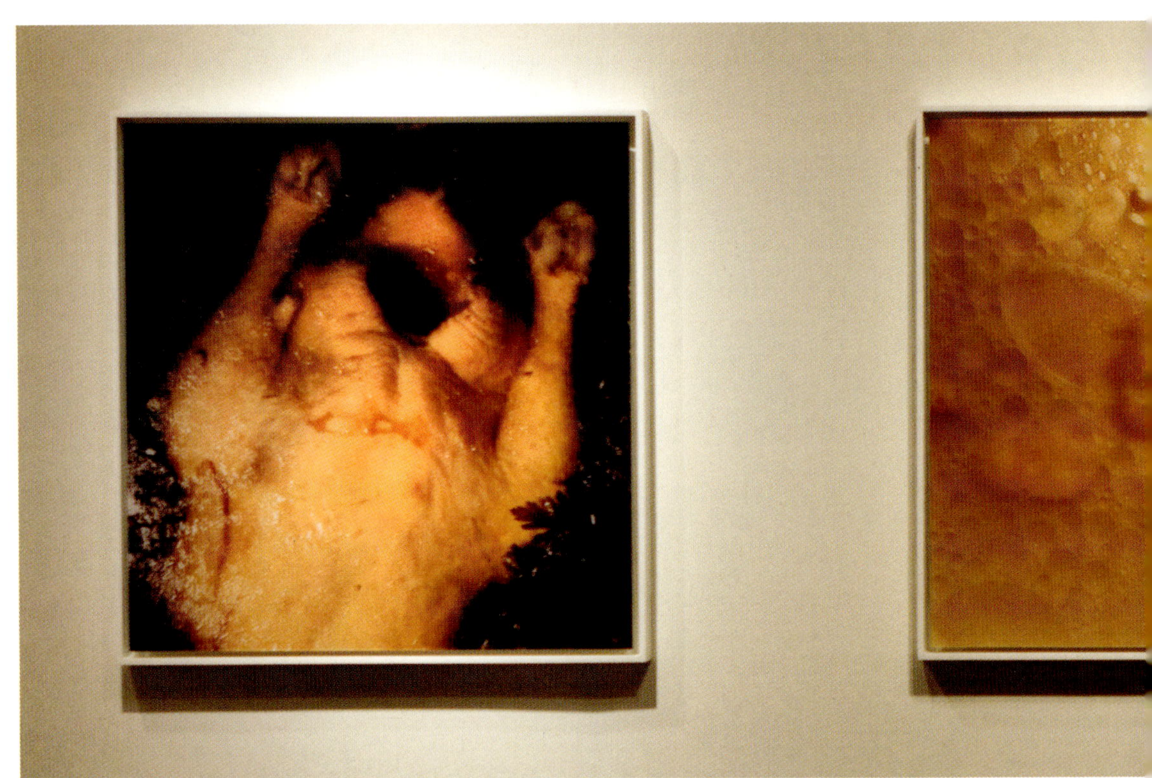

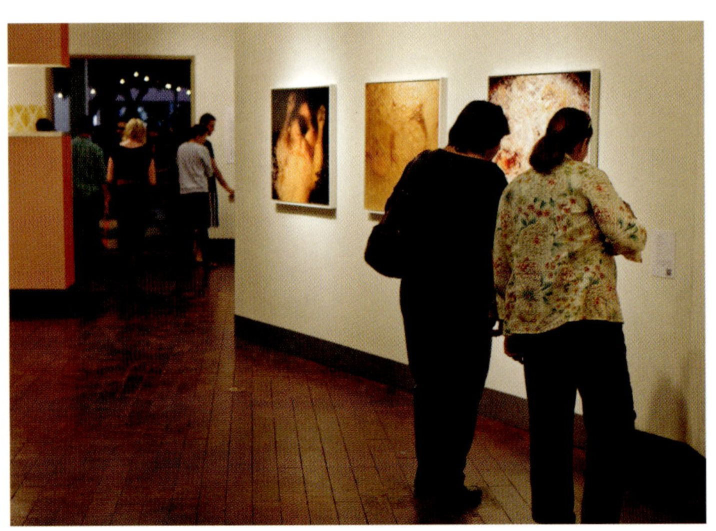

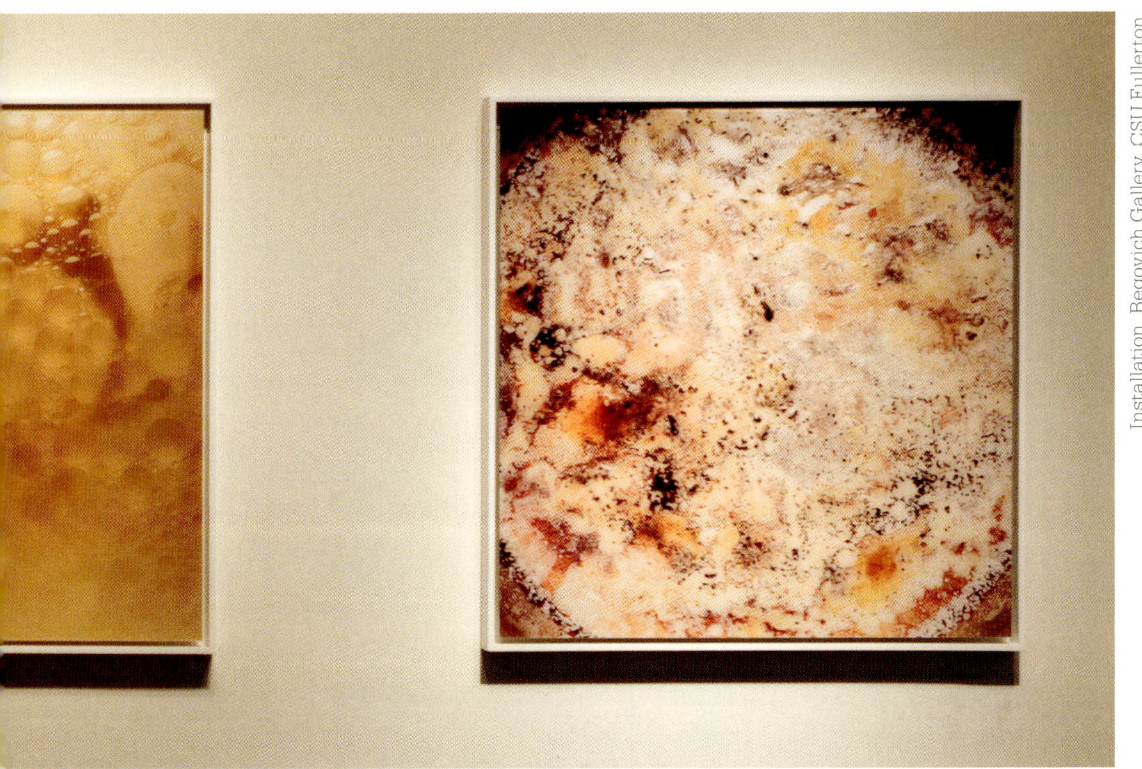

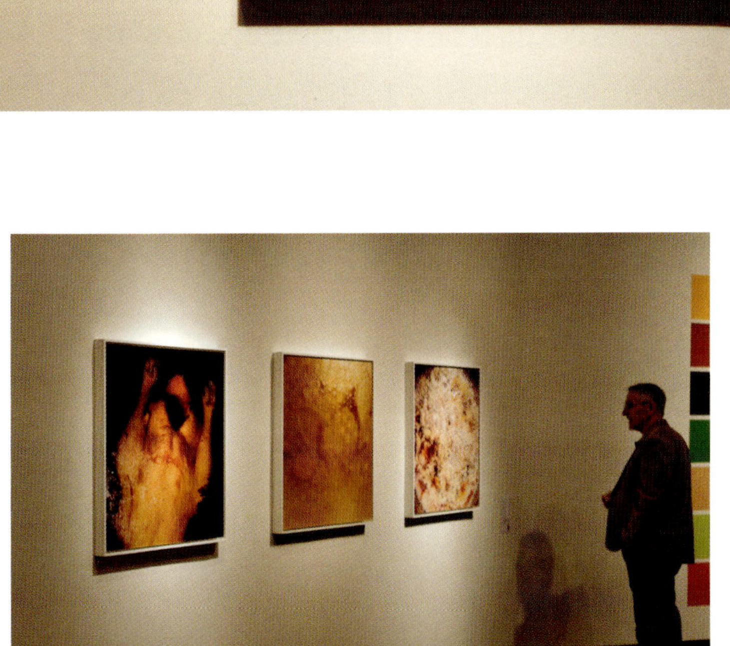

Installation, Begovich Gallery, CSU Fullerton.

JUSTIN PERRICONE

Perricone's artful typography disguises the reality of current trends in consumption of processed foods.

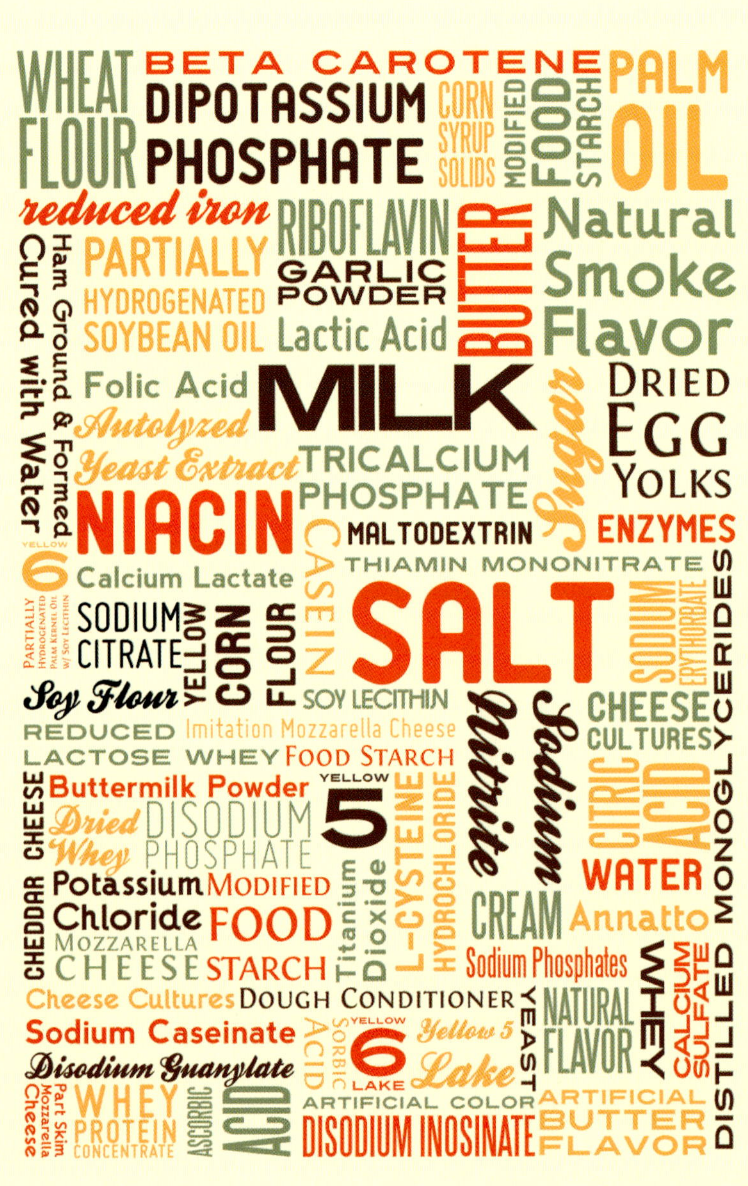

Ham and Cheese Hotpocket Ingredients, 2010. Silkscreen, Artist Proof. 18 x 24 inches. Courtesy of the artist.

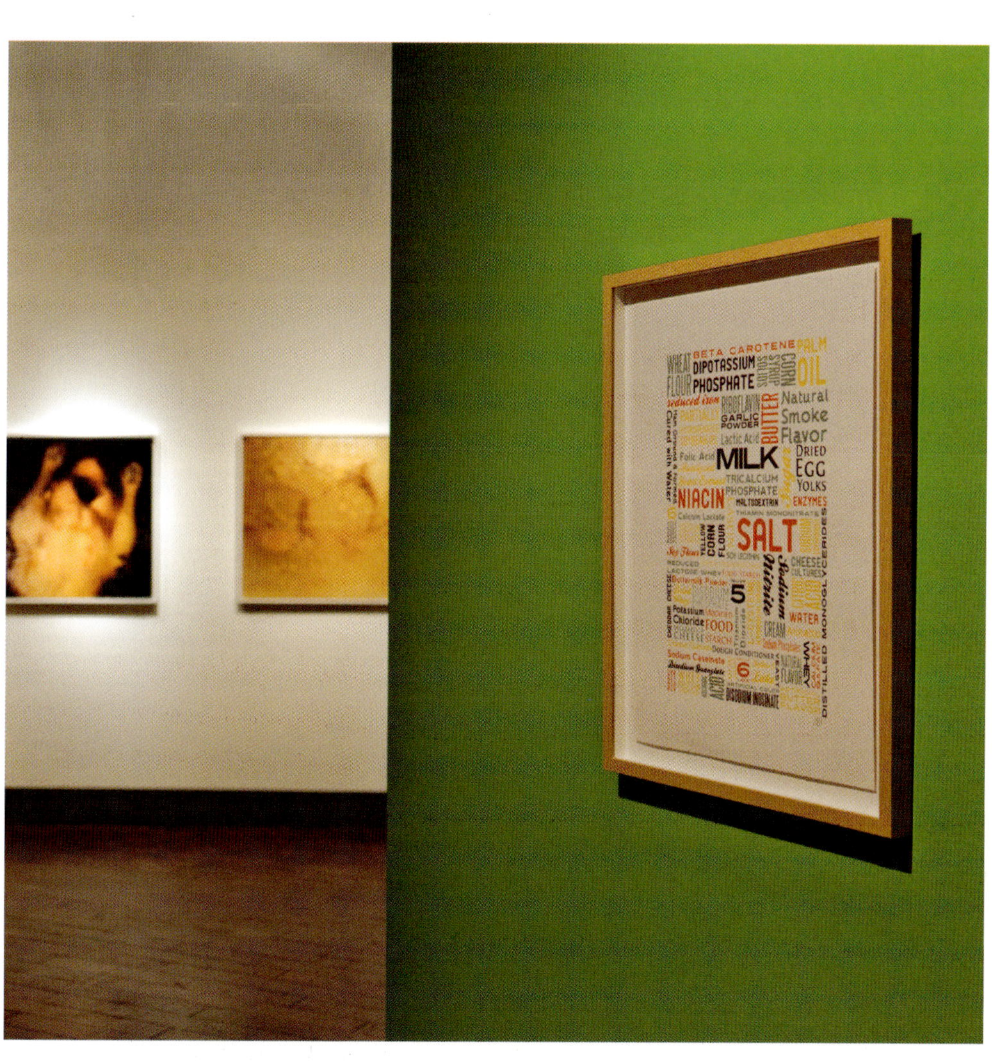

BETA CAROTENE
WHEAT DIPOTASSIUM PALM
FLOUR PHOSPHATE CORN OIL
reduced iron RIBOFLAVIN
GARLIC Natural
POWDER Smoke
Lactic Acid Flavor
Folic Acid MILK DRIED
TRICALCIUM EGG
NIACIN PHOSPHATE YOLKS
MALTODEXTRIN ENZYMES
Calcium Lactate THIAMIN MONONITRATE
YELLOW SALT
CORN
FLOUR SOY LECITHIN
CHEESE
Sodium CULTURES
Nitrite
Buttermilk Powder
5 WATER
Potassium FOOD CREAM
Chloride
CHEESE STARCH
Sodium Caseinate 6
WHEY
DISODIUM INOSINATE

VICTORIA REYNOLDS 

Southern California-based artist Victoria Reynolds paints luscious and sensual renderings of meat. Flesh as a subject matter alludes to all animals, including humans, and our interconnectedness. Recently, she has shifted her focus to abstracted vegetable and fruit imagery as in *Creamed Cherry Crevasse*.

Cartouche of the Resplendent Bung, 2011. Oil on panel. 48 x 36 inches. Courtesy of the artist.

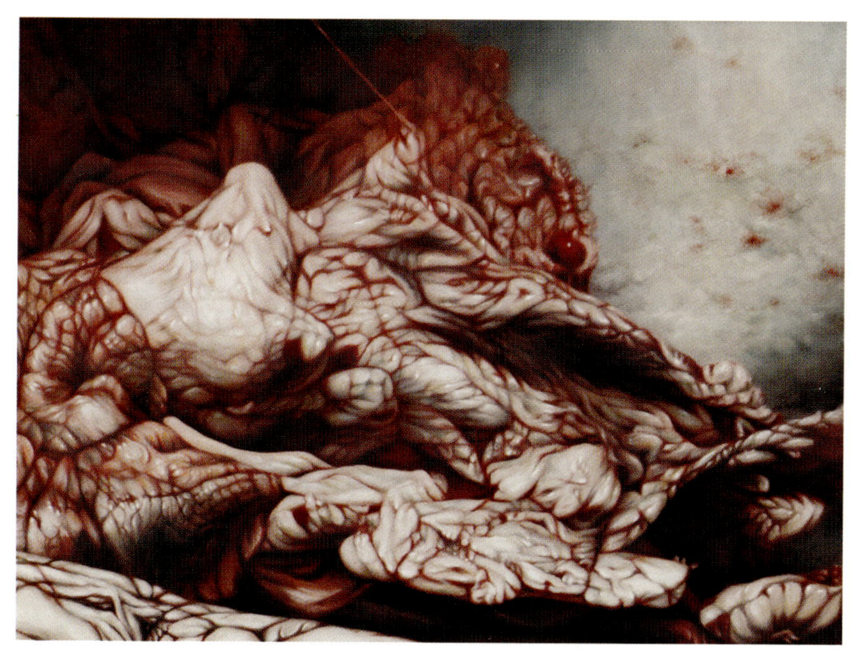

Reindeer Slope, 2008-10. Oil on panel.
48 x 36 inches. Courtesy of the artist.

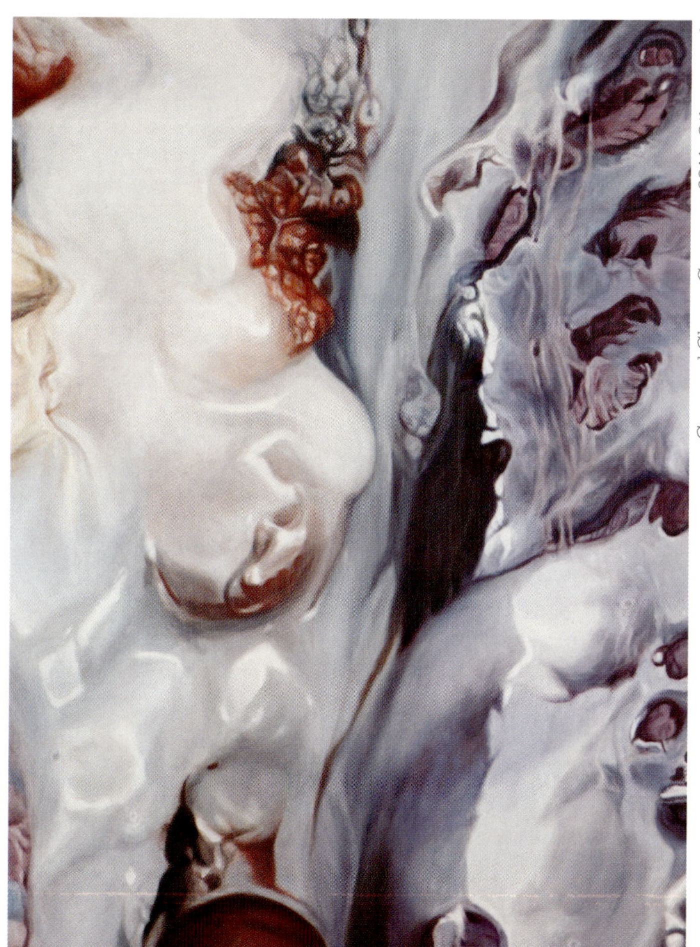

Creamed Cherry Crevasse, 2011. Oil on panel.
32 x 24 inches. Courtesy of the artist and Richard Heller Gallery.

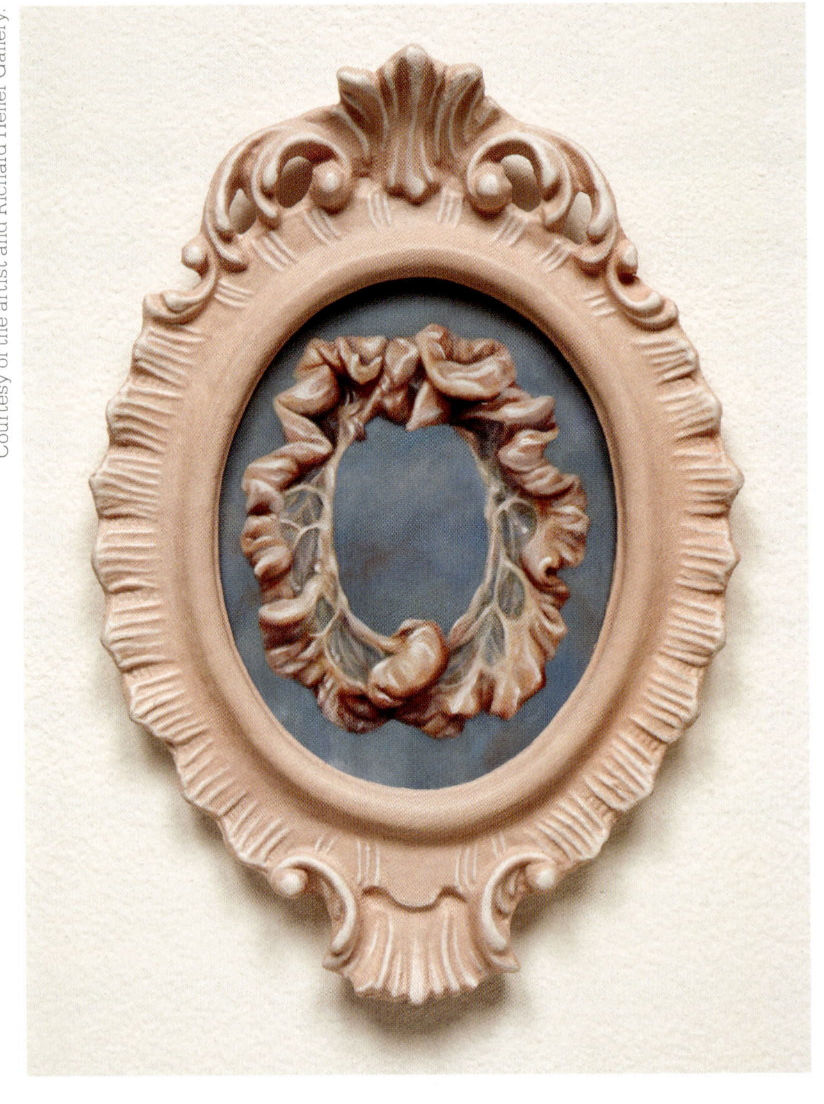

Uteral Coil. 2010. Oil on panel. 8.5 x 6 inches.
Courtesy of the artist and Richard Heller Gallery.

JENNIFER RUBELL 

Rubell's work fuses the provocative and the playful. Meshing art historical references, sexual taboos and double entendres, Rubell invites the viewer to participate in an action that is irreverent and revealing.

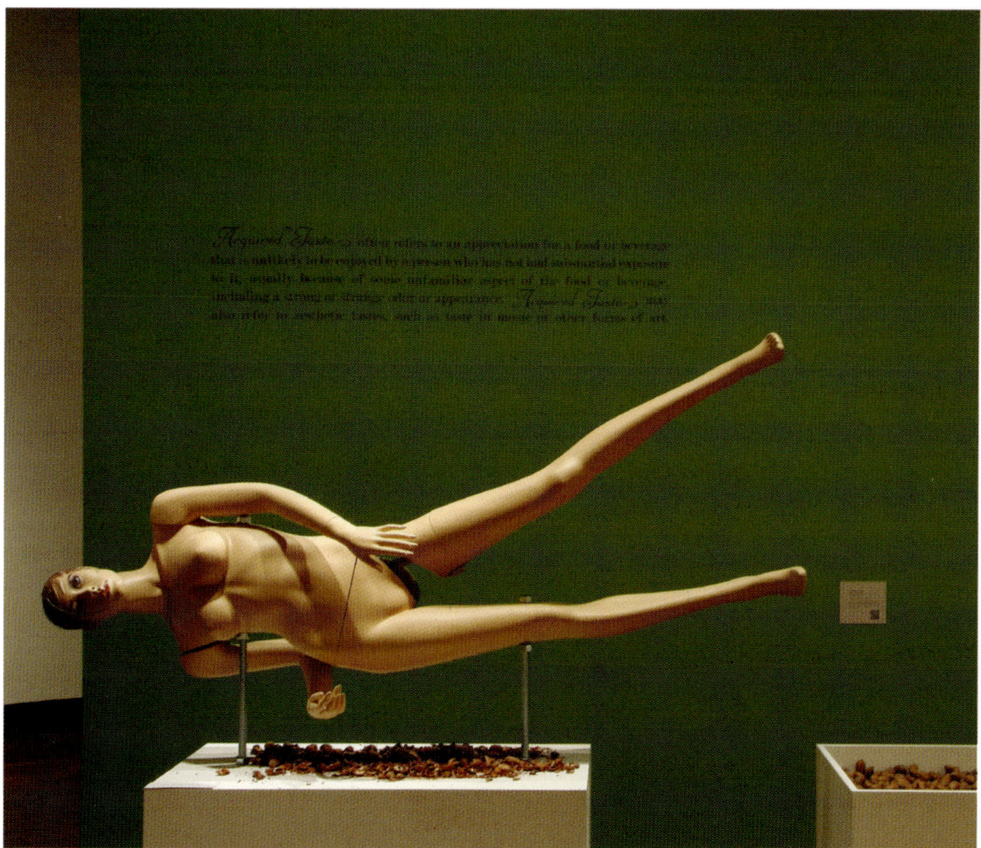

Nutcracker (Lucy), 2011. Fiberglass, metal, wood paint, pecans. Dimensions variable. Courtesy of Stephen Friedman Gallery.

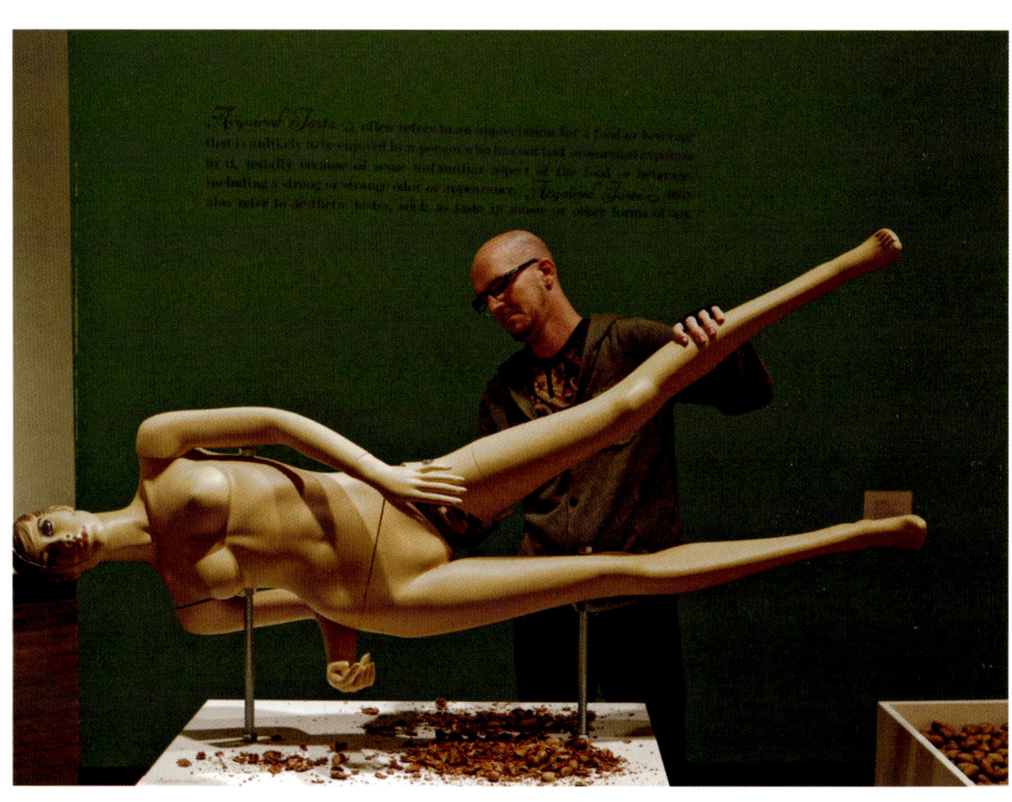

Acquired Taste is often refers to an appreciation for a food or beverage that is unlikely to be enjoyed by a person who has not had substantial exposure to it, usually because of some unfamiliar aspect of the food or beverage, including a strong or strange odor or appearance. Acquired Taste may also refer to aesthetic tastes, such as taste in music or other forms of art.

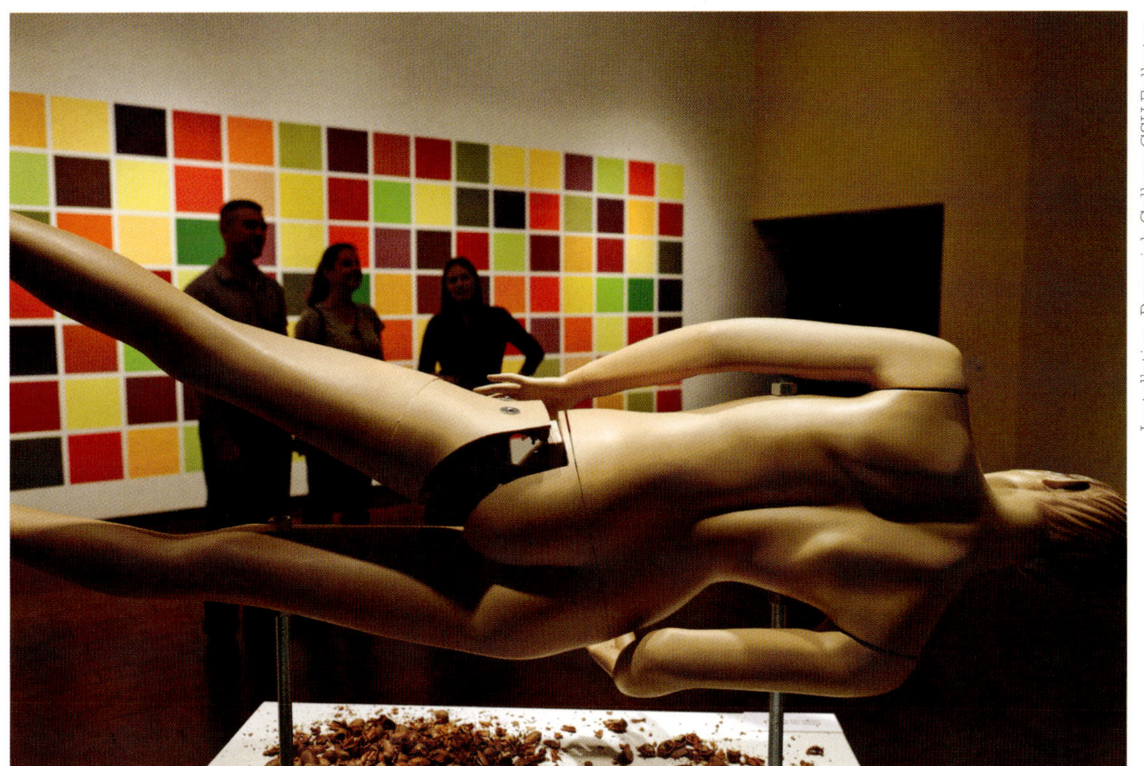

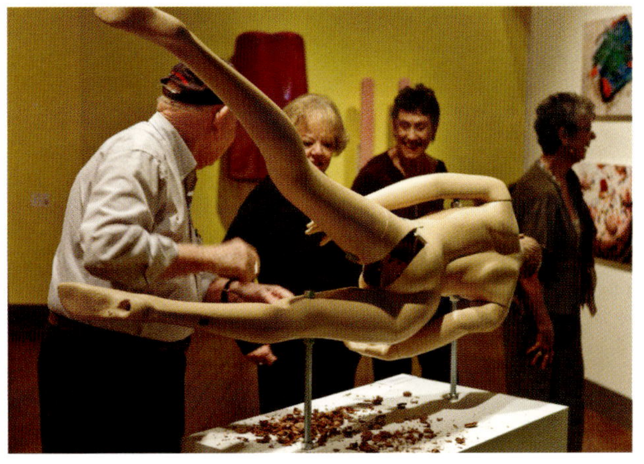

Installation, Begovich Gallery, CSU Fullerton.

STEPHEN j SHANABROOK

While working in a morgue, Shanabrook made casts of mortal wounds from trauma victims, later crafting individual chocolates from these wounds. Straddling the line between surrealism and entropy, *Wedding Favors* reminds us all that brutality and beauty are often inextricably tied together.

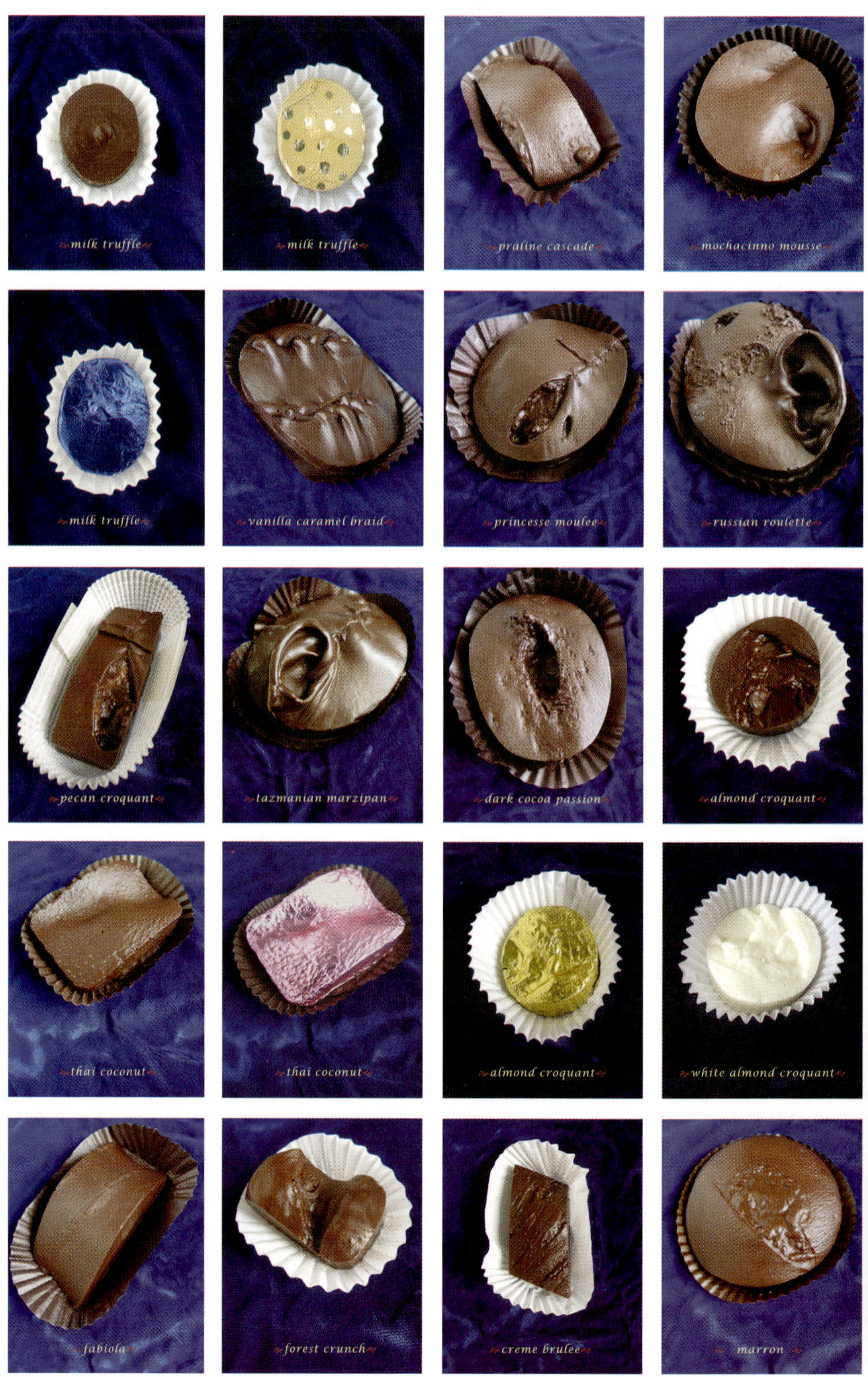

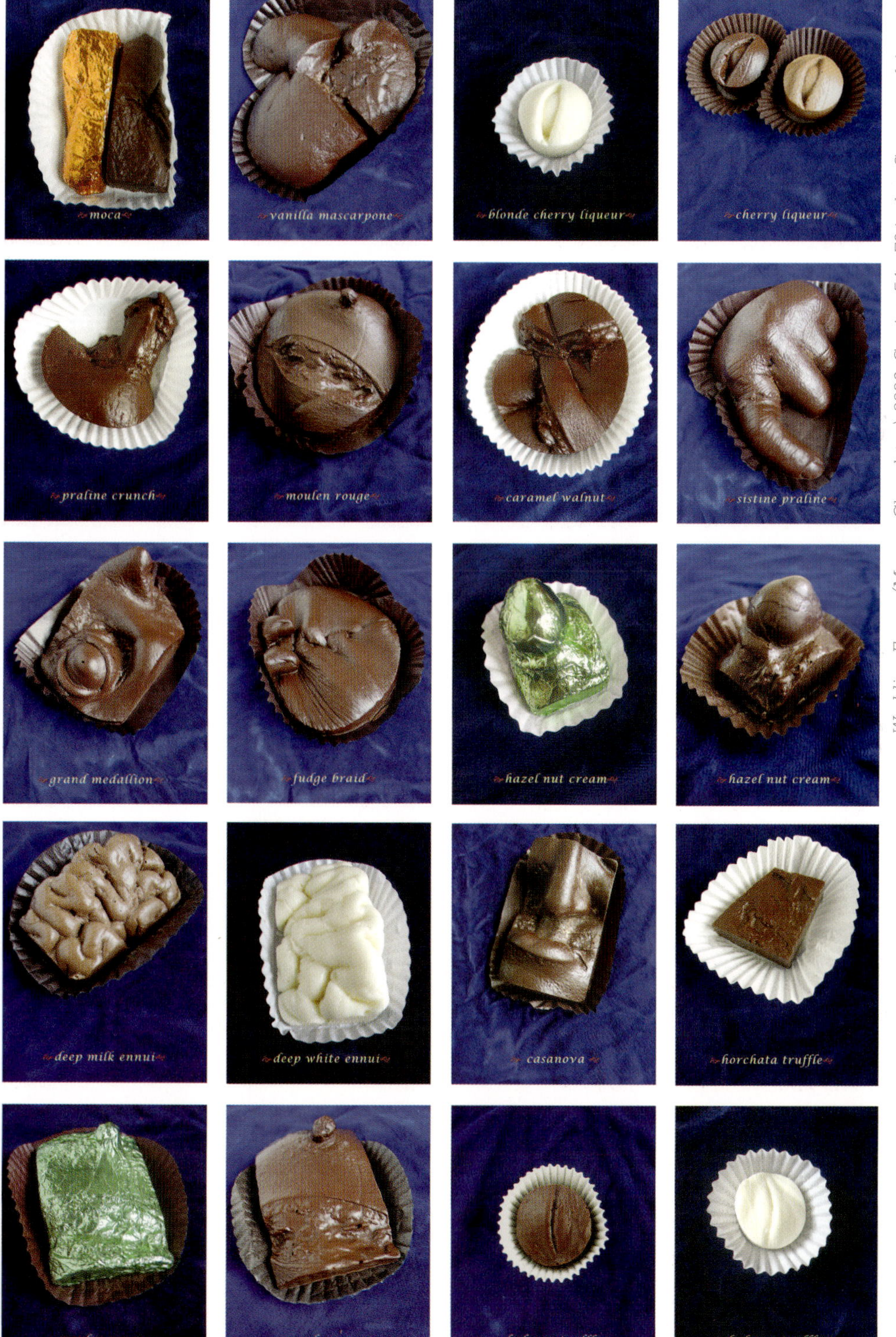

Wedding Favors (Morgue Chocolates), 2006. C-print. 54 x 70 inches. Courtesy of the artist.

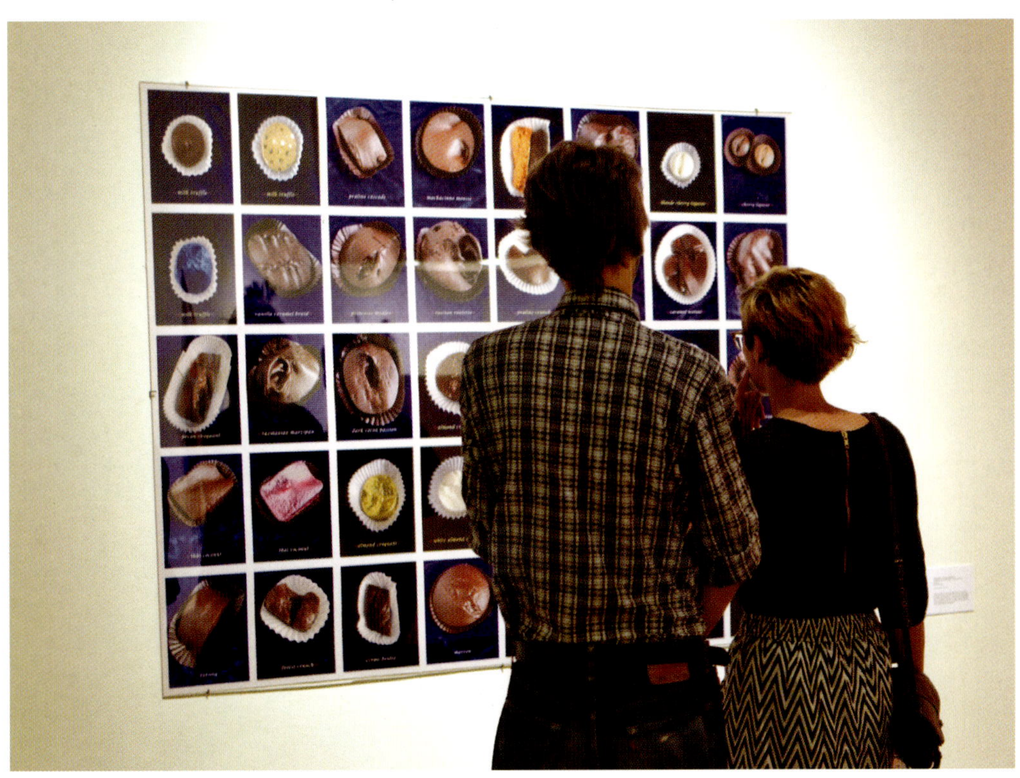

Operating on the edge of surreal and disturbing, Shanabrook's *Hopping Hills* transforms a banal childhood memory, the chocolate Easter bunny, into a disquieting commentary on addiction.

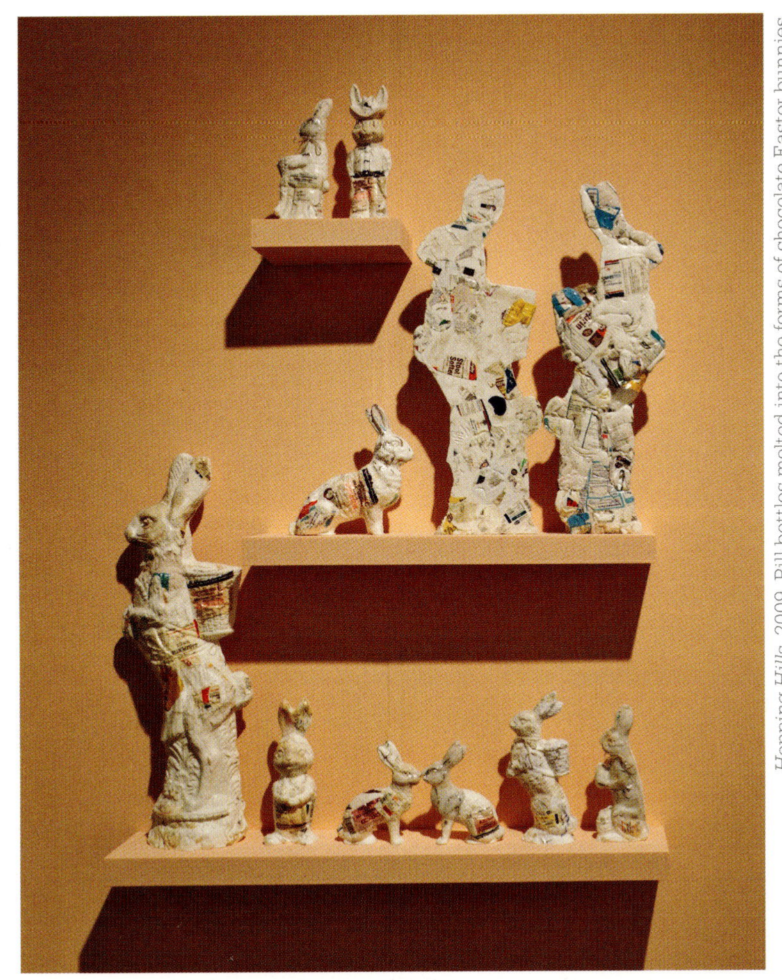

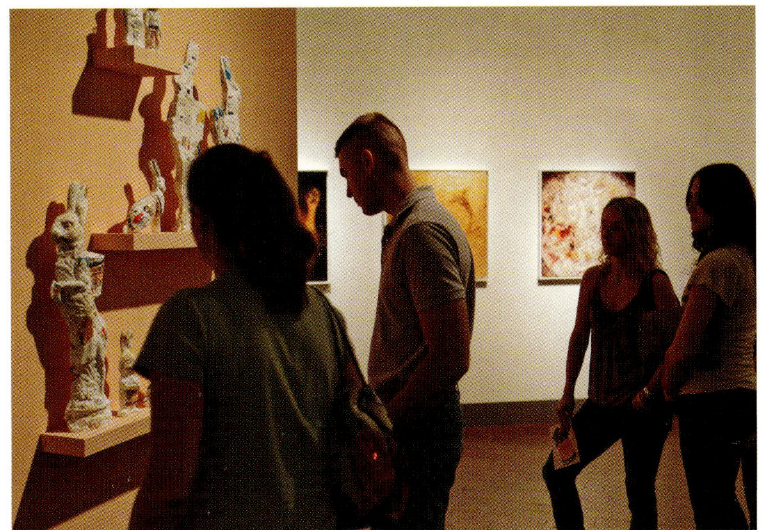

Hopping Hills, 2009. Pill bottles melted into the forms of chocolate Easter bunnies. Dimensions variable. Courtesy of the artist.

GREG STEWART

Stewart's *On The Edge Is Decorated With Carvings* body of work was created during his residency with the CSUF Begovich Gallery and CSUF Grand Central Art Center. While in California, he traveled to the Salton Sea, where he photo-documented his performance. His performances, sculptures, and documentation imagine the future of sustainability and agriculture within an urban context: for example, a suit that grows fig trees, genetically modified pigs which can grow apples, and a portable garden on wheels.

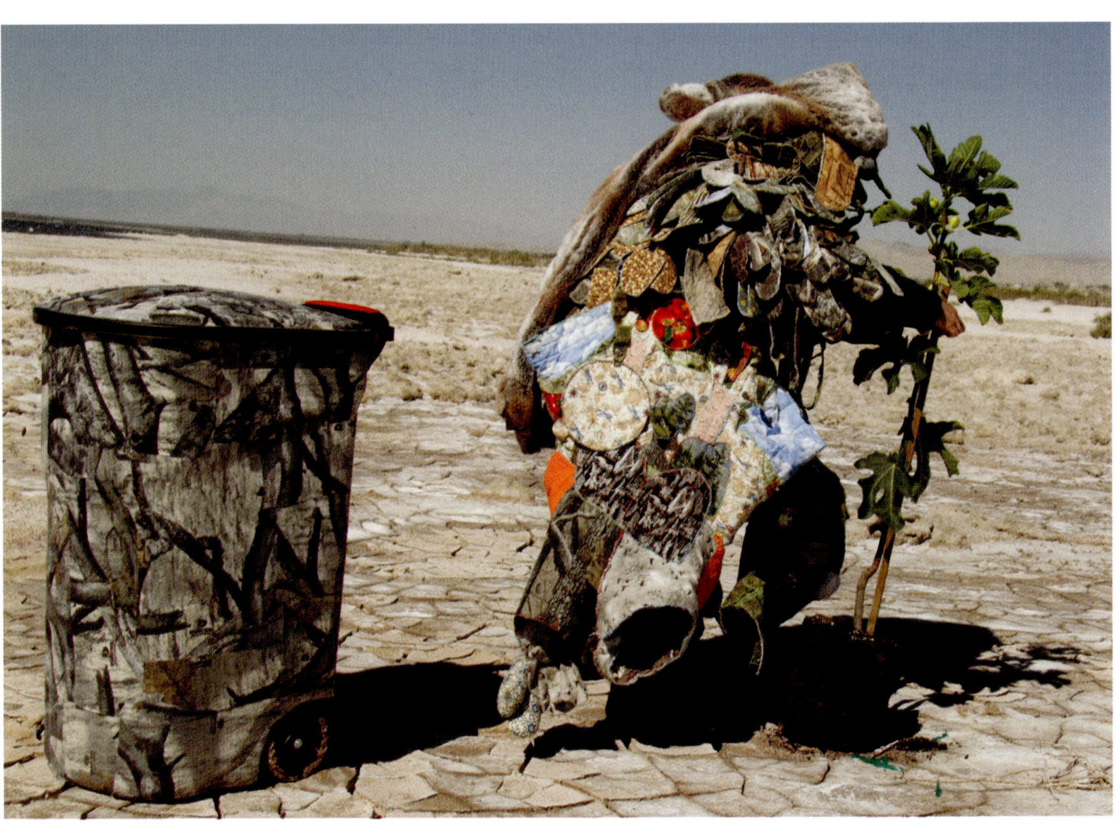

On The Edge Is Decorated With Carvings: Salton Sea (Photo-documentation), 2011. Digital photography. Dimensions variable. Photographs by Angelica Perez.

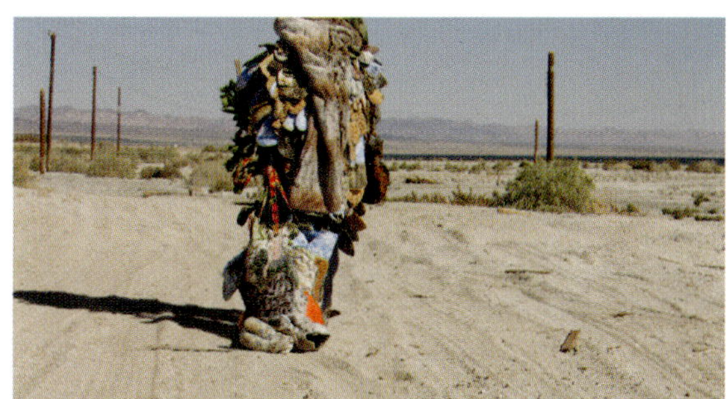 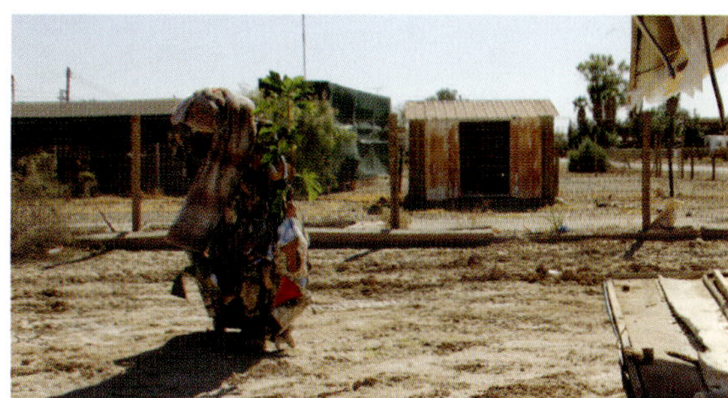

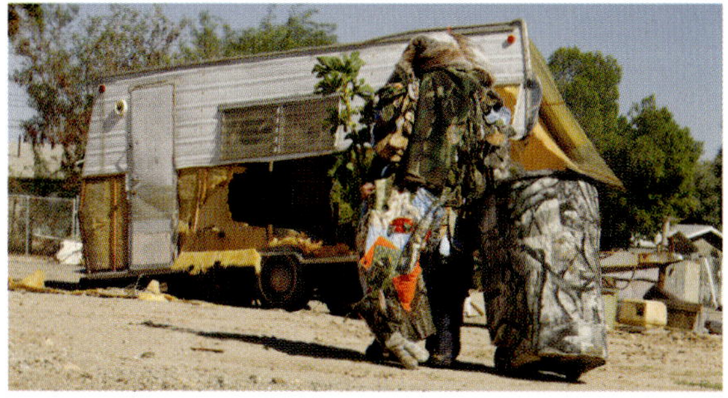 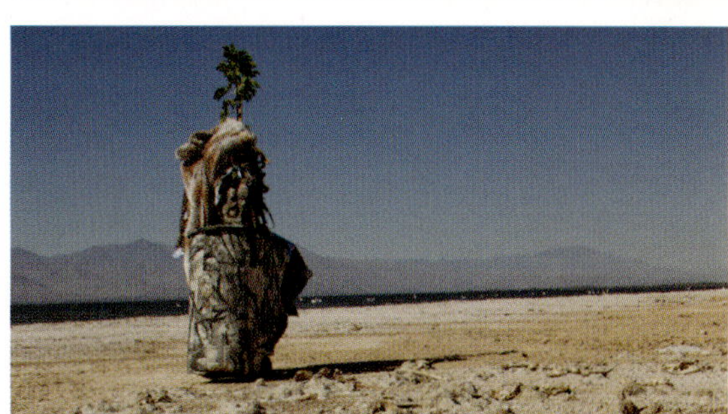

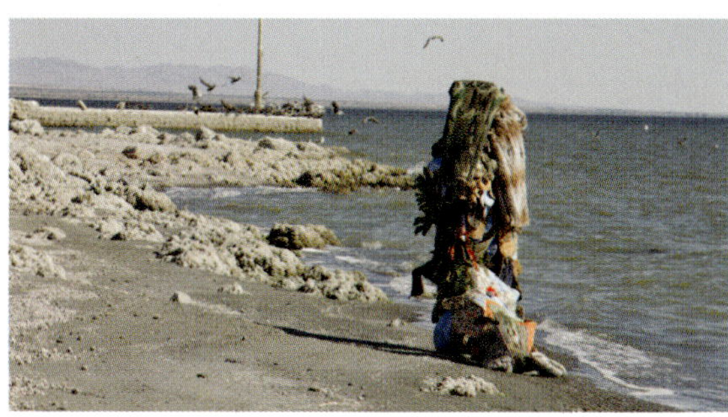 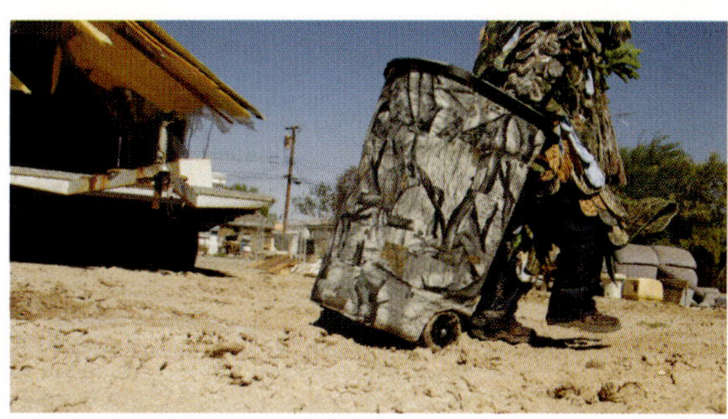

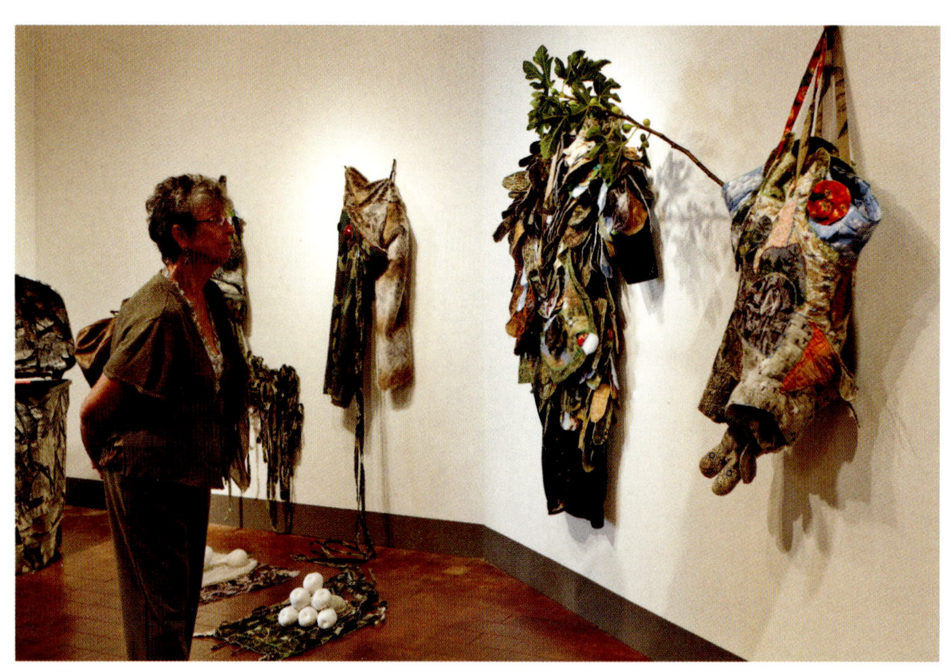

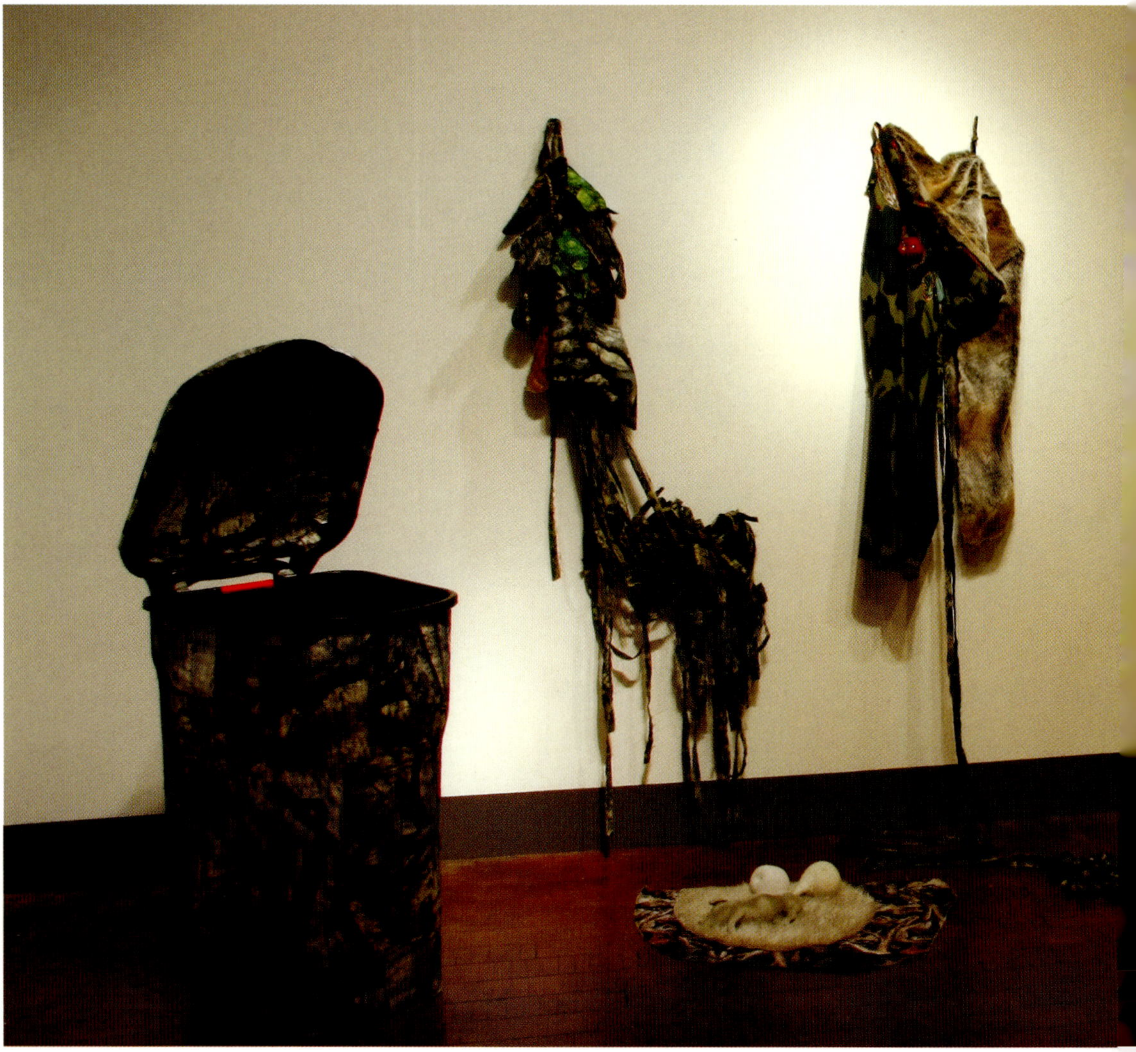

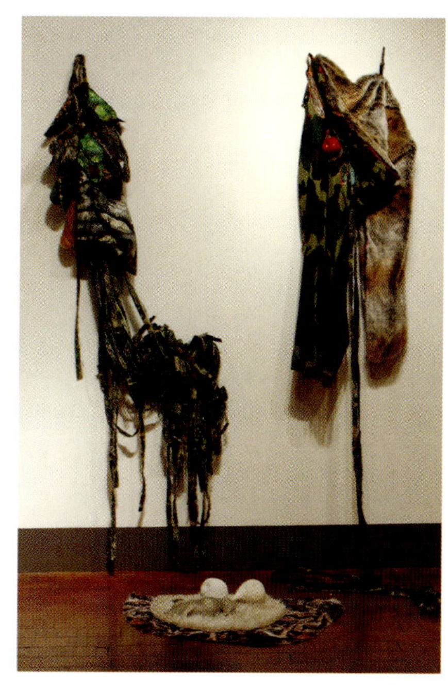

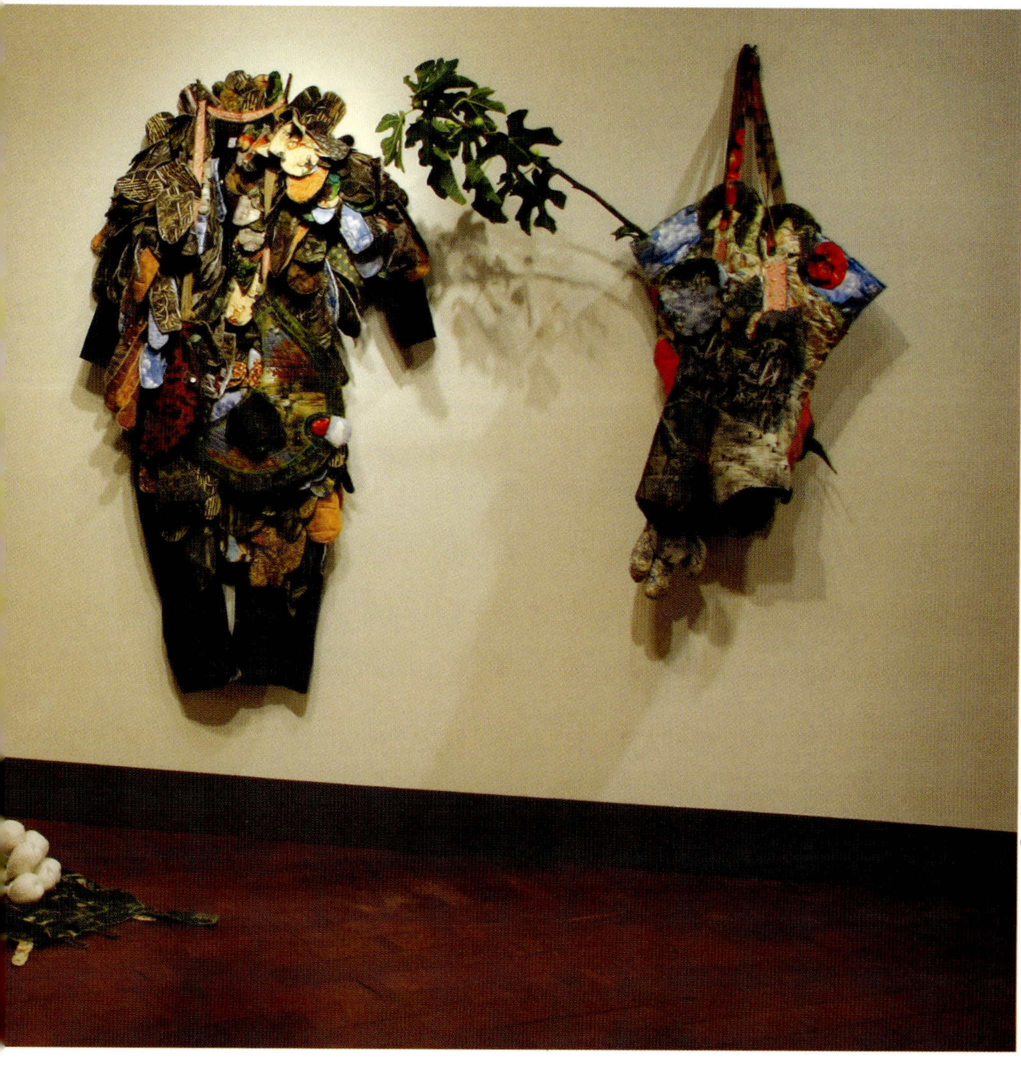

On The Edge Is Decorated With Carvings: Contentious Invention (Pigs). 2011. Mixed media.
Dimensions variable. Courtesy of the artist.

TATTFOO TAN 

Tan's *Nature Matching System* is a community and participatory art project created as a reminder to consume your daily recommended doses of color. Each square is matched to the color of a fruit, vegetable, or edible plant.

Mural Artists: Jason Chakravarty, Alyssa Cordova, S.A. Hawkins, Joanne Mace, Kimberly McKinnis, Conception Rodriguez, Heather Richards-Siddons, Brent Siddons, Allison Town, Emily Darman Allen Tyler, Patricia Reed

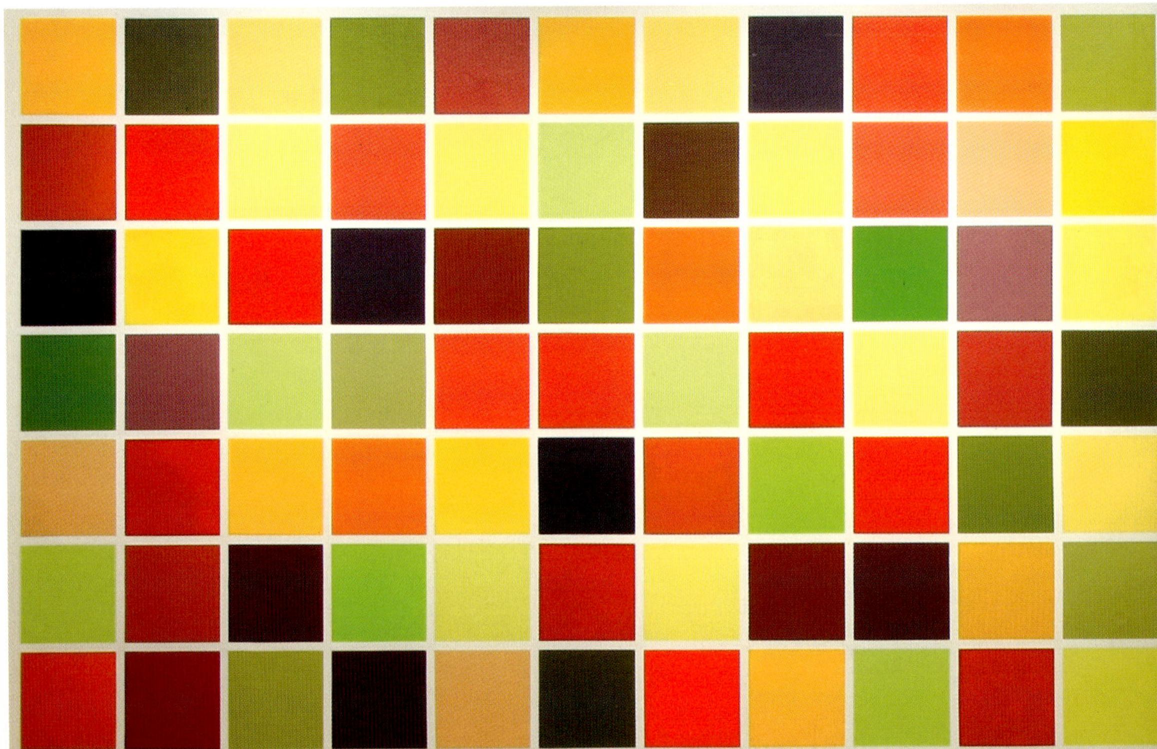

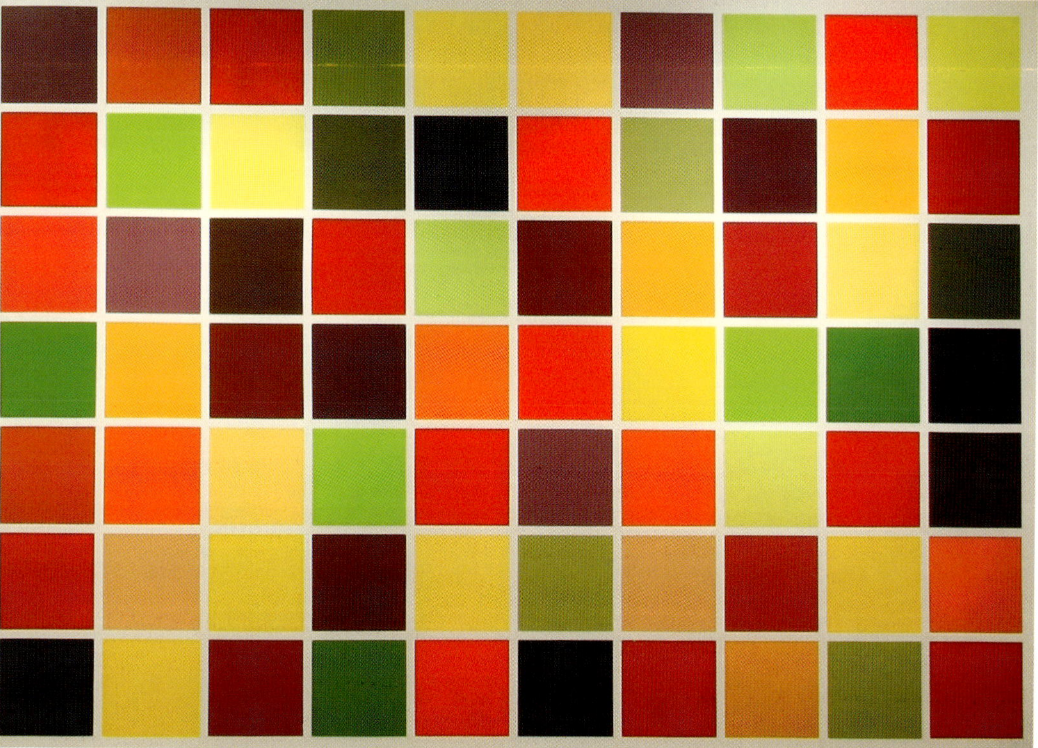

Nature Matching System, 2011. Community Mural Project. Acrylic house paint. 12 x 37.5 feet.

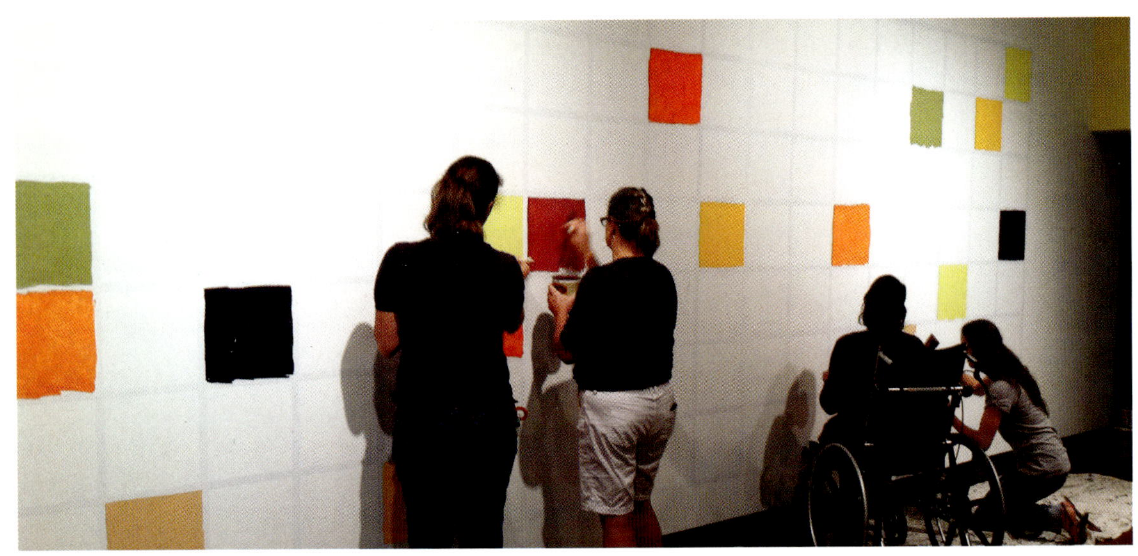

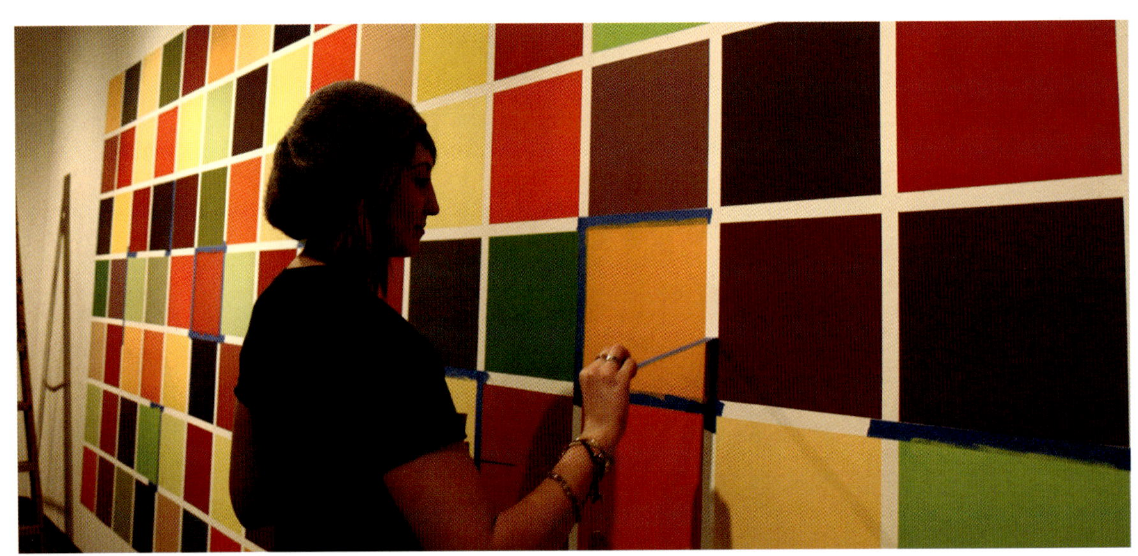

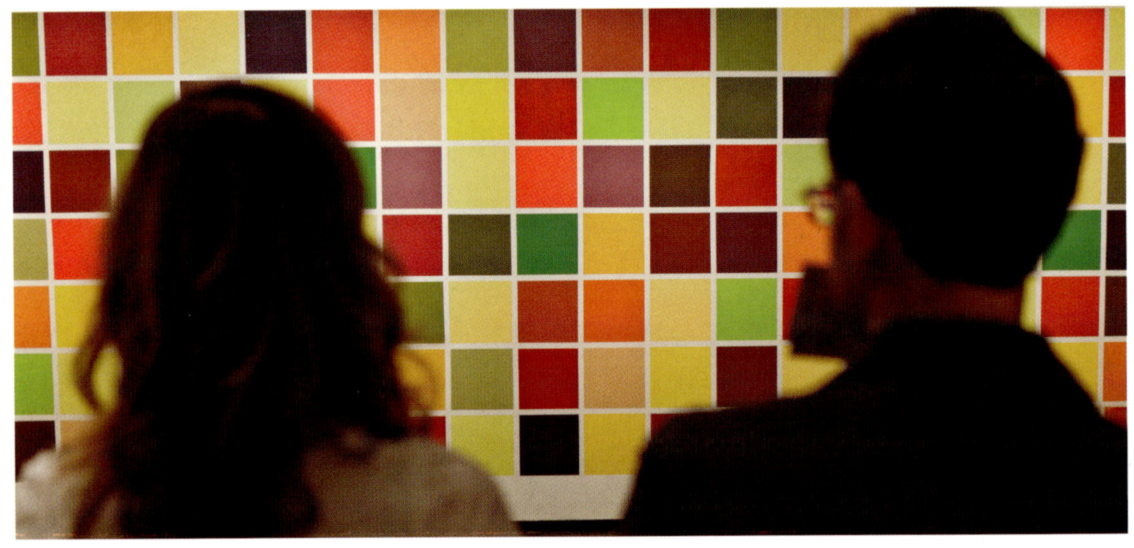

INSTALLATION PHOTOGRAPHS

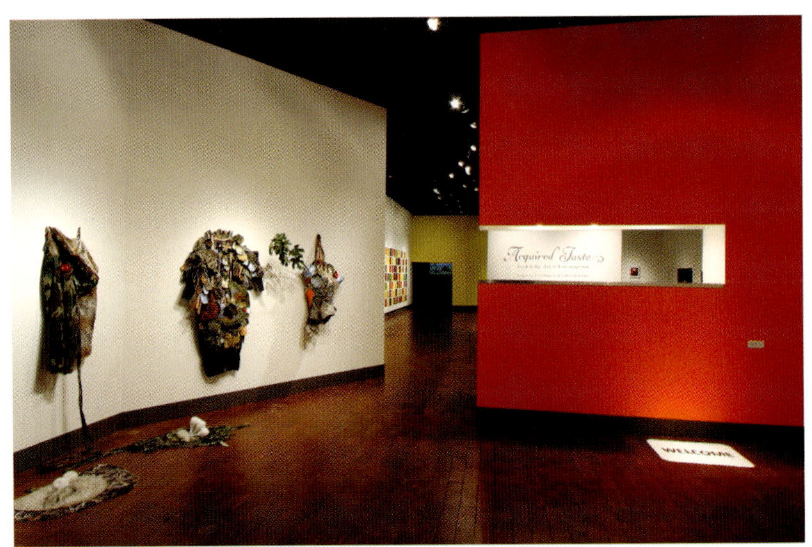

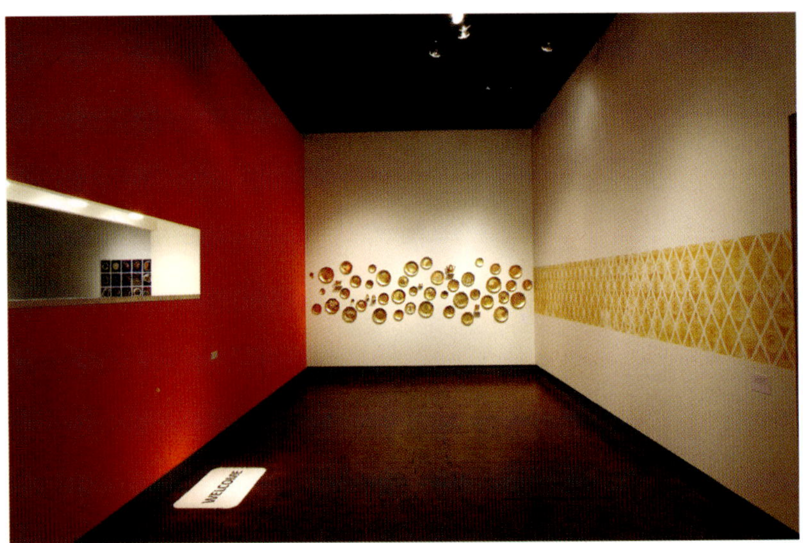

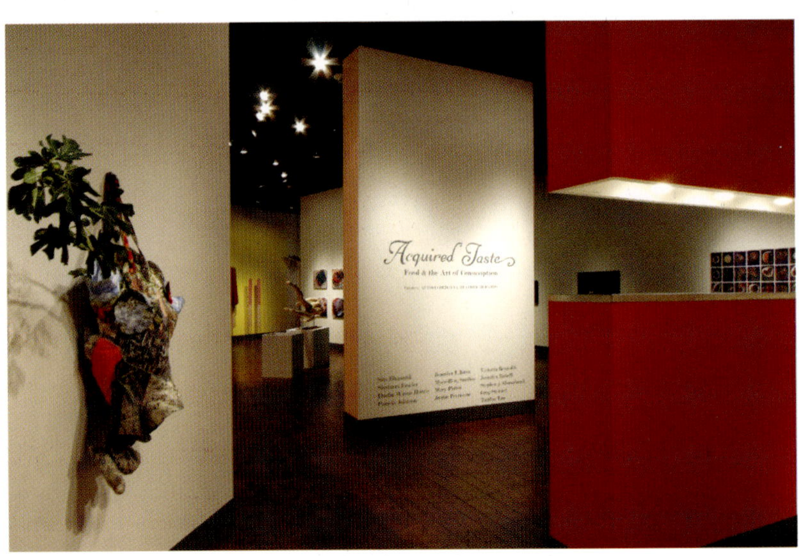

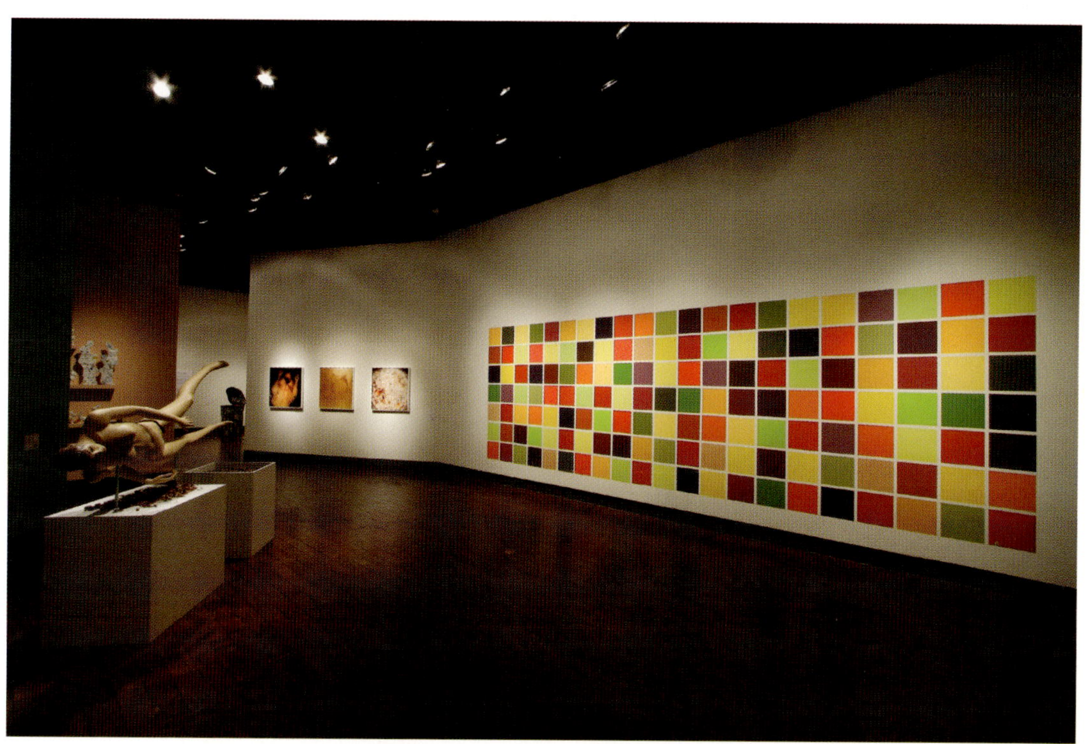

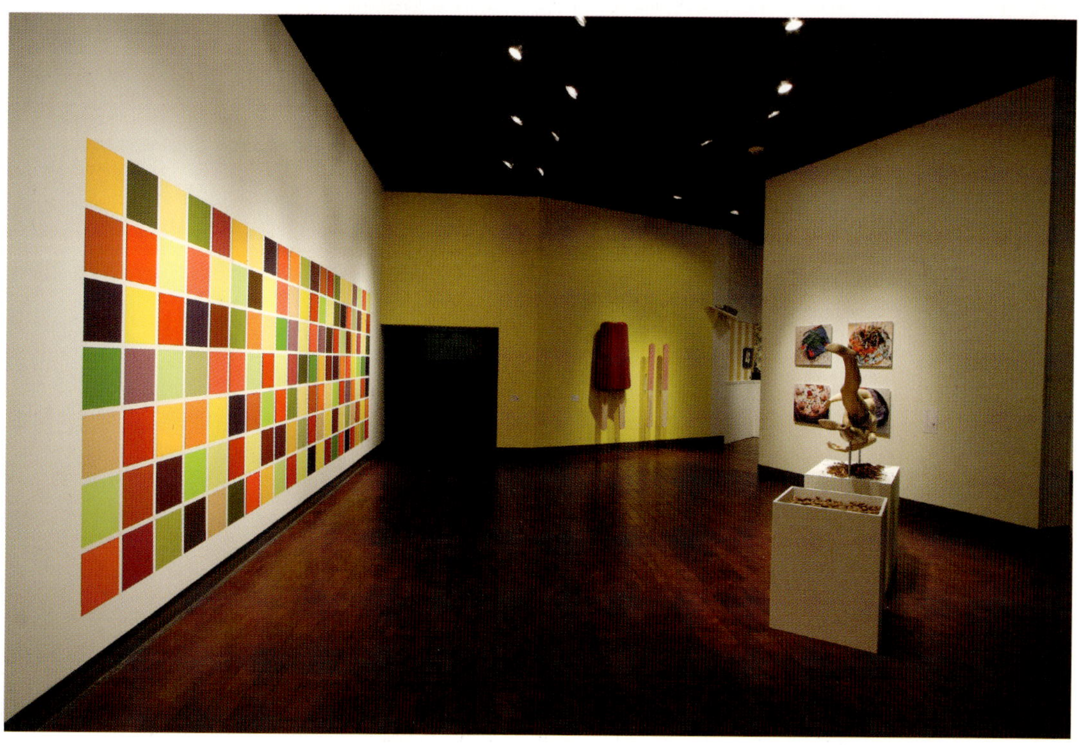

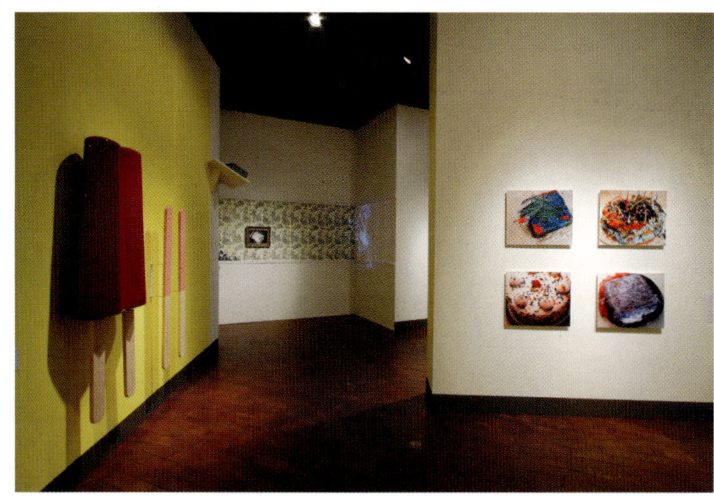

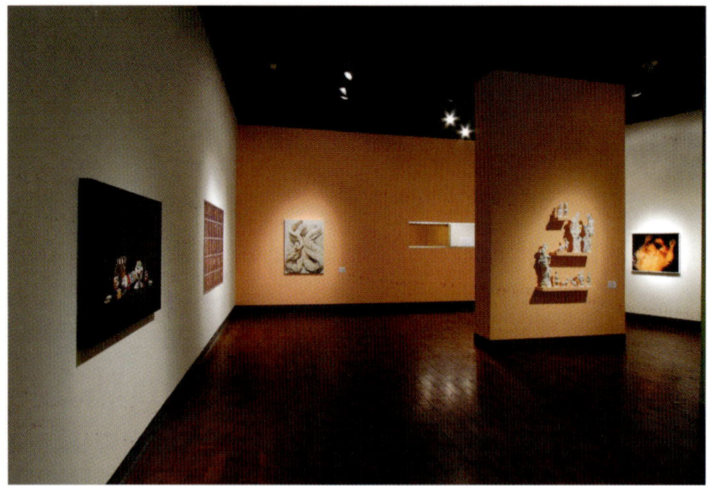

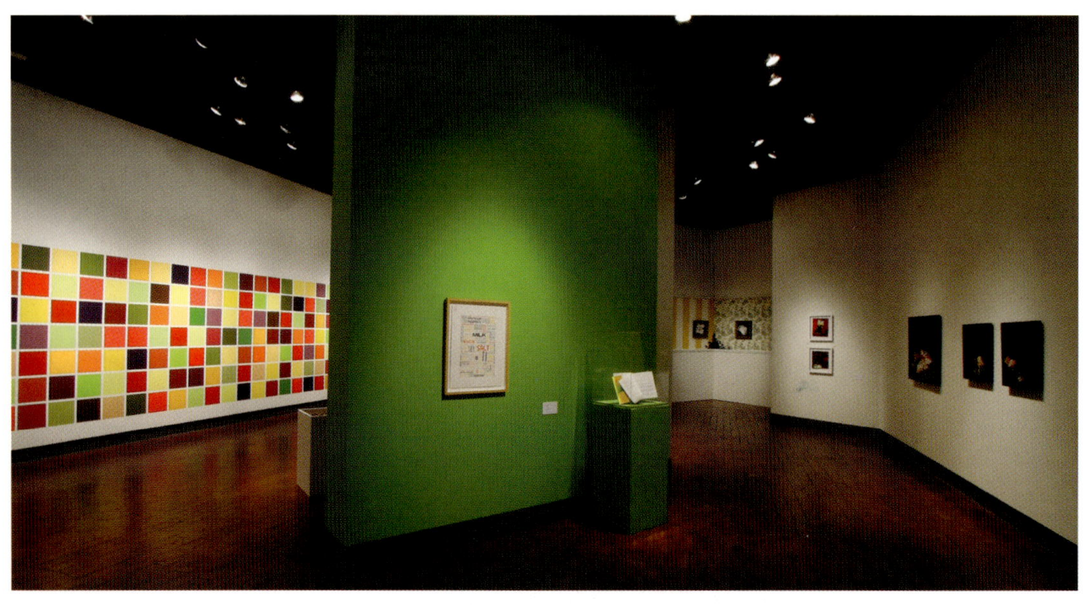

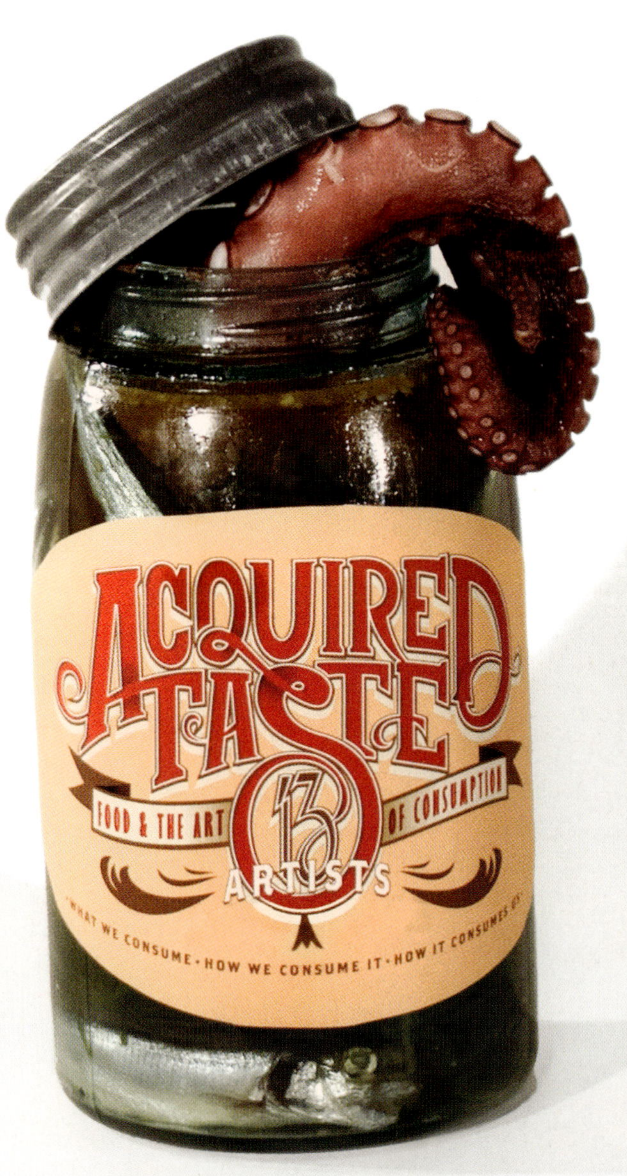
ACQUIRED
TASTE
13
FOOD & THE ART
OF CONSUMPTION
ARTISTS
"WHAT WE CONSUME · HOW WE CONSUME IT · HOW IT CONSUMES US"

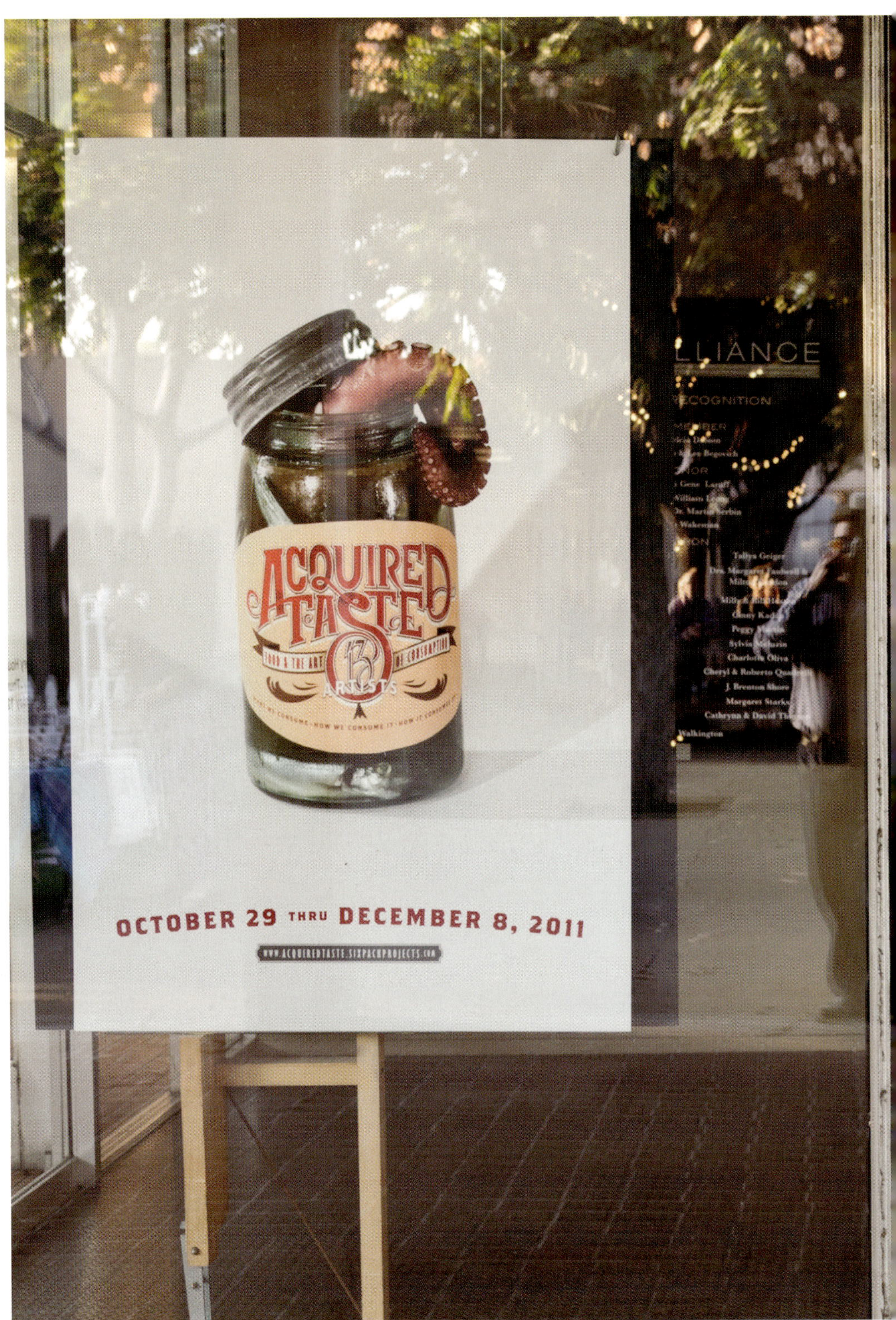
ACQUIRED TASTE
FOOD & THE ART OF CONSUMPTION
13 ARTISTS
OCTOBER 29 THRU DECEMBER 8, 2011
WWW.ACQUIREDTASTE.SIXPACKPROJECTS.COM

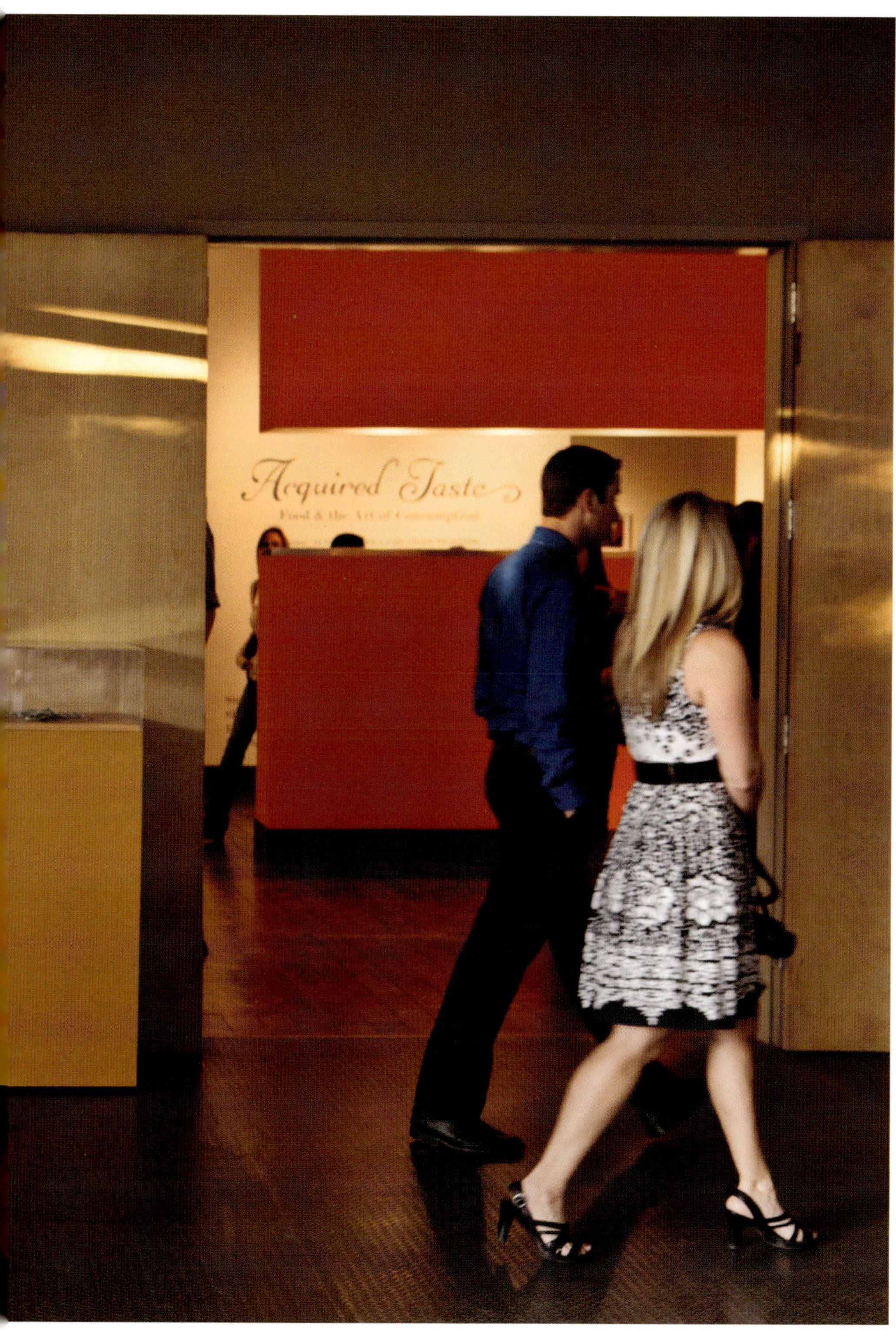

Acquired Taste
Food & the Art of Consumption

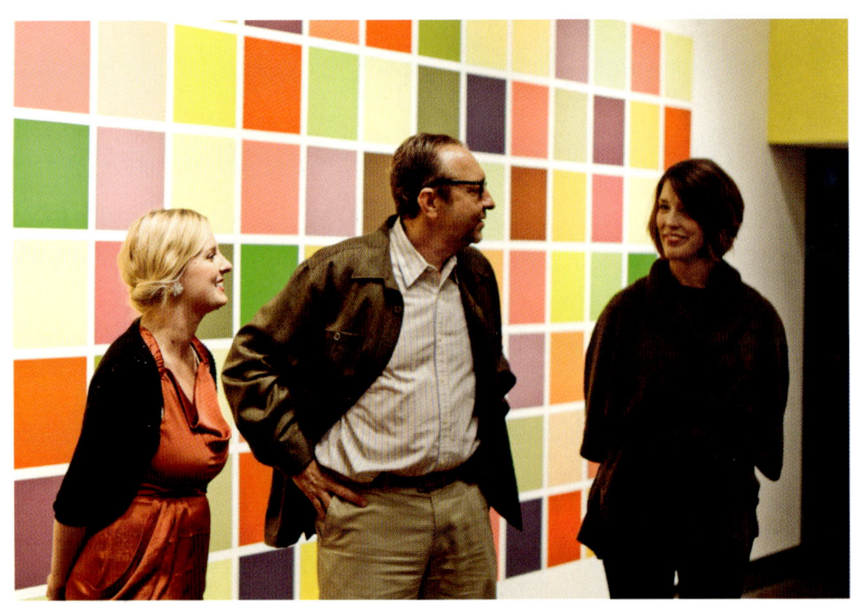

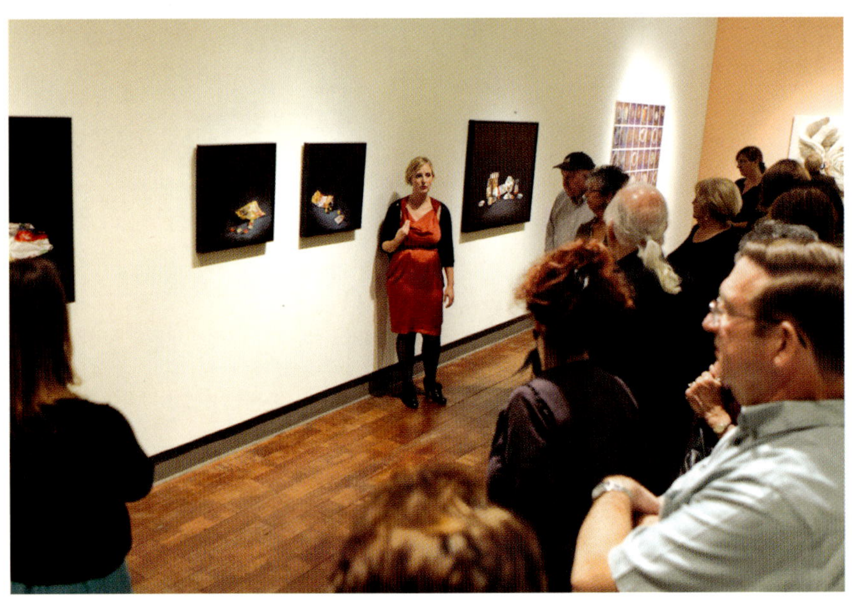

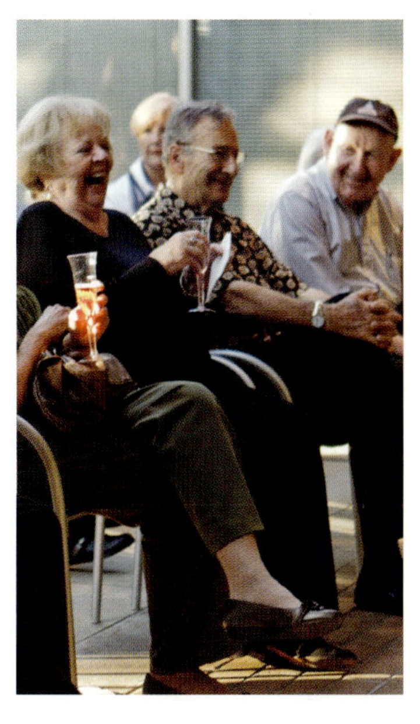
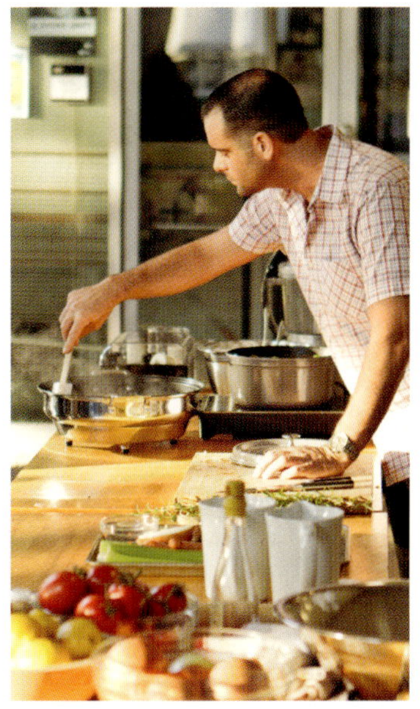
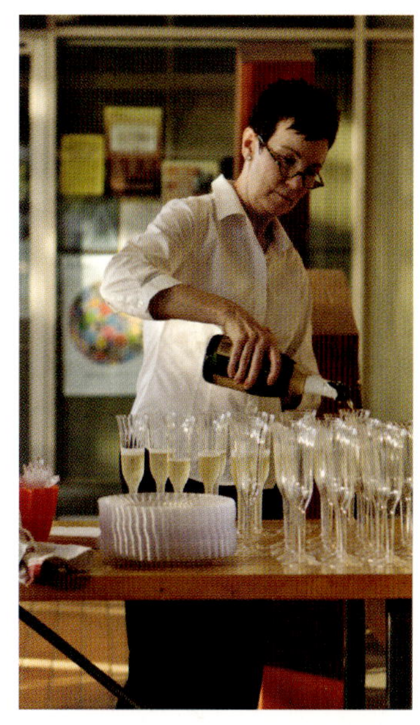
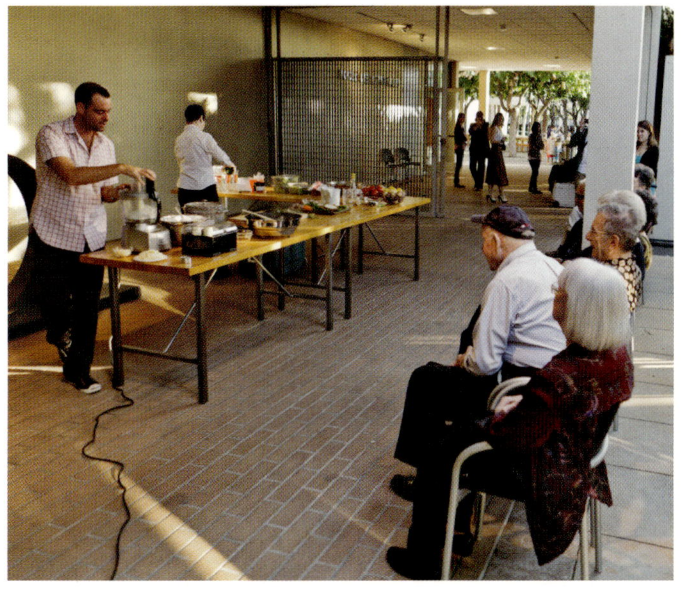
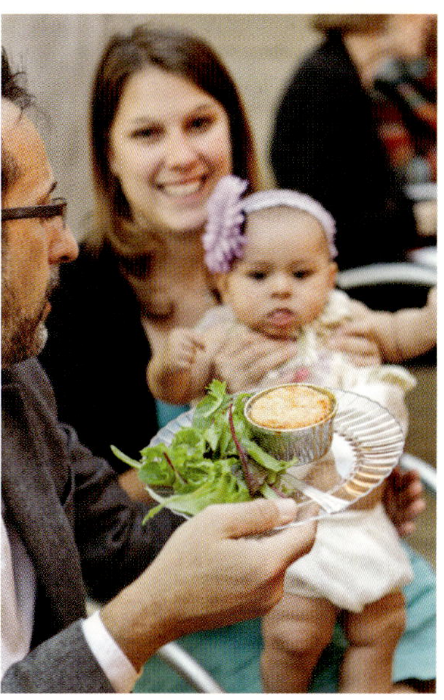

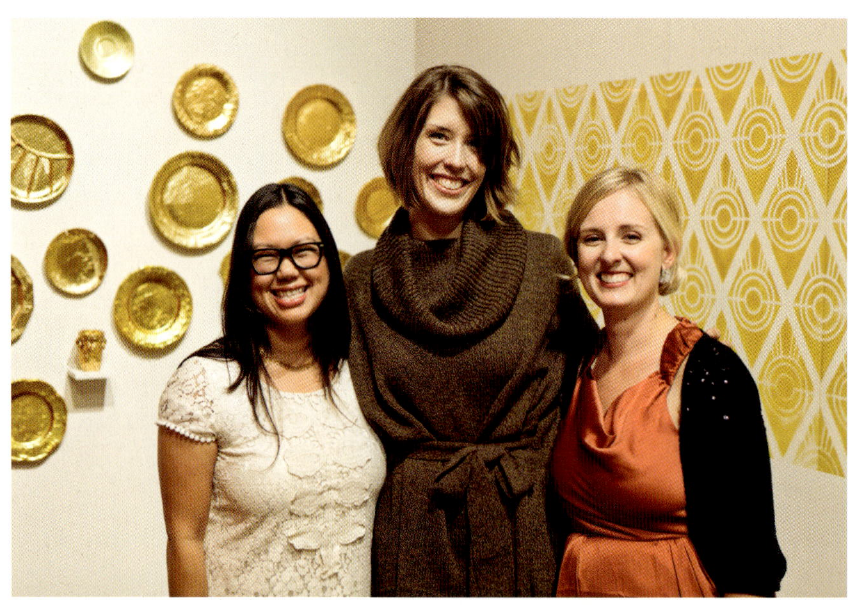

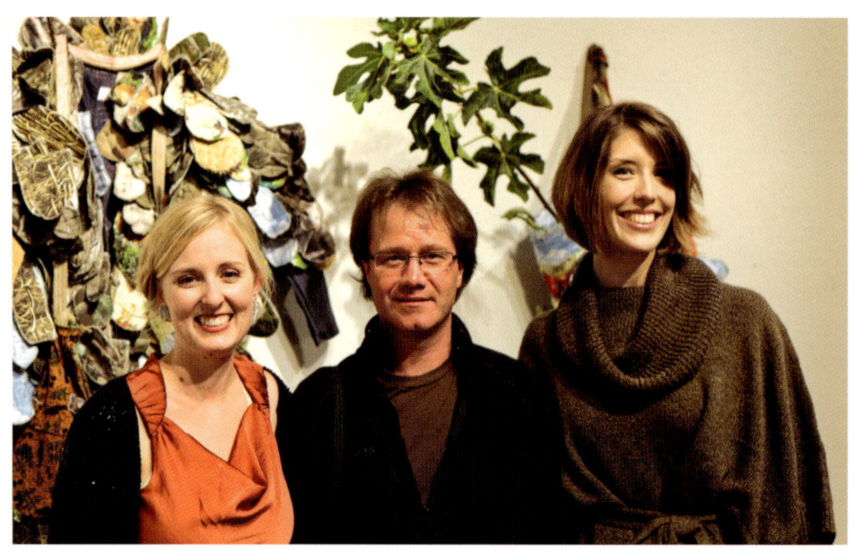

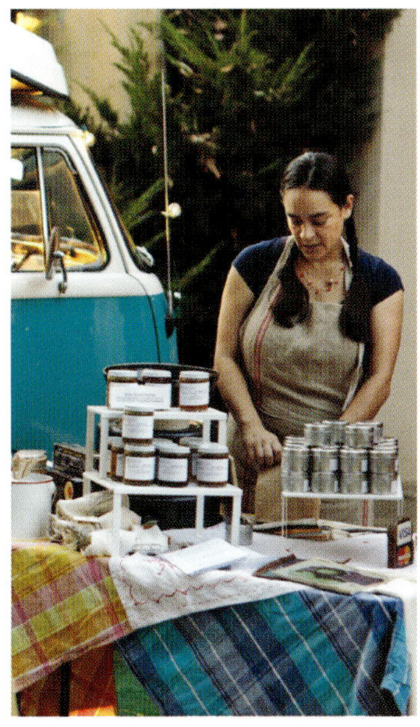
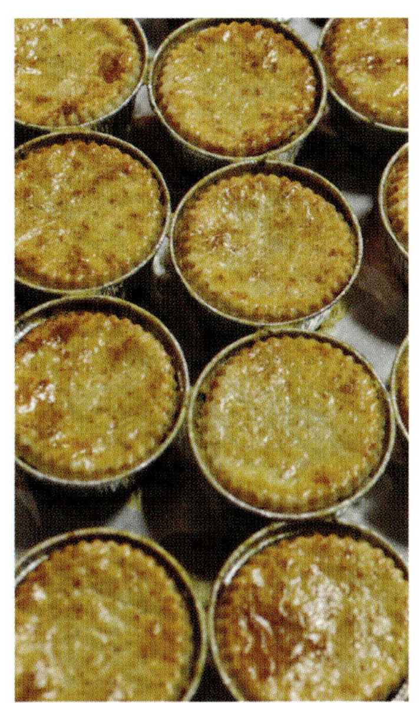
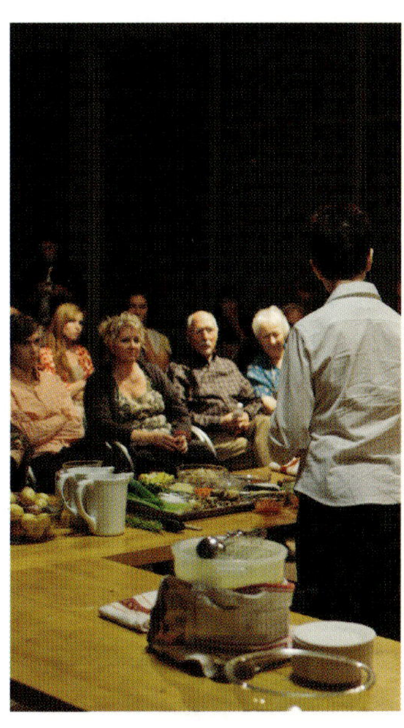

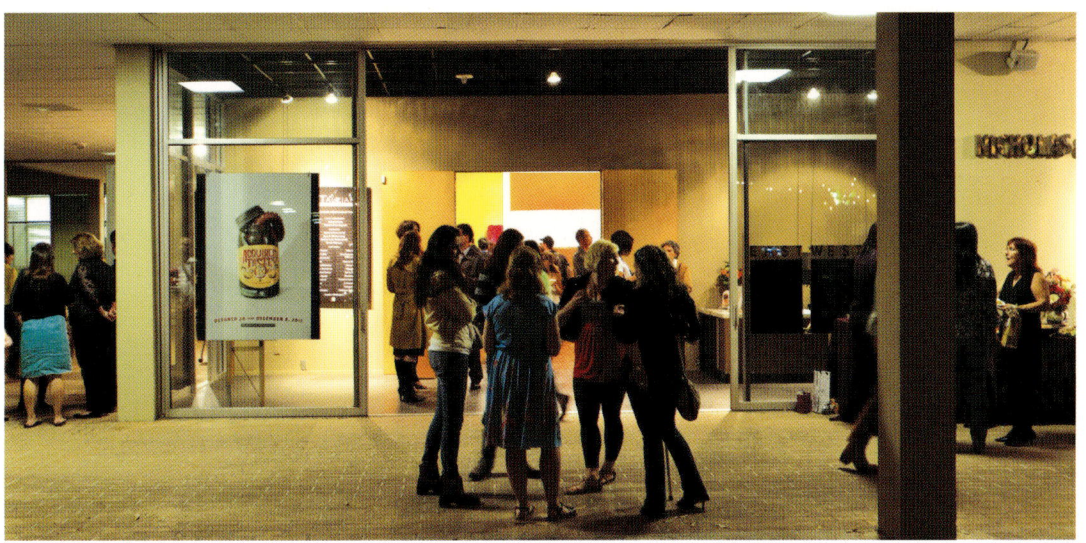

RECIPES

Jonathan Dye

Chef and culinary instructor Jonathan Dye was invited to create original recipes inspired by the work of several of the artists in *Acquired Taste: Food and the Art of Consumption*: Dustin Wayne Harris, Mary Parisi, Victoria Reynolds, Jennifer Rubell, Artist-in-Residence Greg Stewart, and Tattfoo Tan. In the exhibition, these artists were denoted by a Quick Response (QR) code, a two-dimensional digital barcode designed to be read by smartphones and other digital devices, which was printed on each artist's wall label. When scanned, the QR code then directed the user to the *Acquired Taste* website, where they could browse these recipes.

Dye also re-created some of these delicious and creative recipes at the opening reception for *Acquired Taste* (if you were able to grab a mini chicken pot pie, consider yourself lucky!). In addition, many of the appetizers and desserts served, generously made by foodie friends and co-workers, were also clever interpretations of the artwork in the exhibition.

DATE CRUMBLE
DUSTIN WAYNE HARRIS

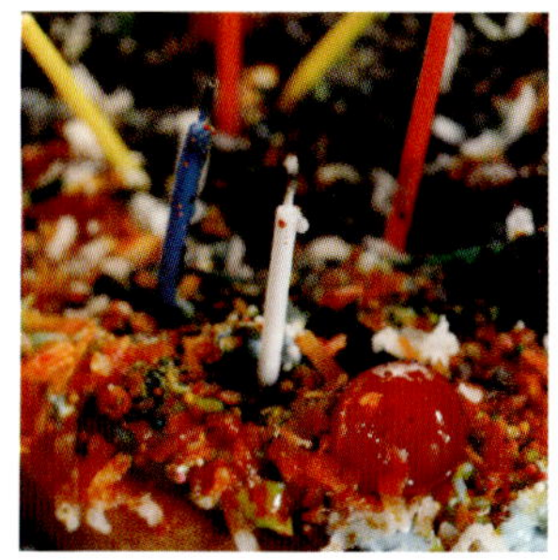

This recipe was passed on to me by my grandmother and is no doubt a basic recipe that could be whipped up in a matter of minutes and likely given to her by her church buddies. What I do love about the recipe is the dates. While dates may be outmoded, they reserve a special place in my heart as something sweet, chewy, and versatile for desserts or savory dishes. This may not be a "date" cake, but who hasn't experienced a crumbled date before? I know I have…before my very own eyes.

CHICKEN POT PIE WITH LEMON AND THYME
MARY PARISI

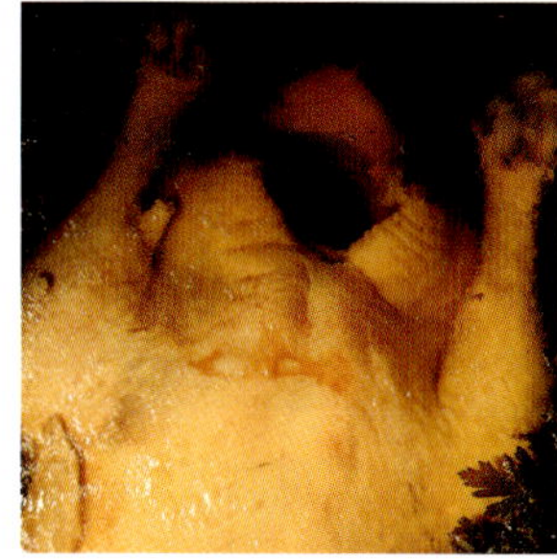

This single-crust pie is the something that feeds your heart with warmth and memory, and piques your interest with a few twists and turns. Growing up with Swanson's Pot Pies, I decided to break out of the shell and try multiple recipes that would deliver just the right touch. This is the pie that was at the end of my journey. Gently cooked and focused on quality ingredients, it may be my favorite fall meal. If pie crust frightens you, make the filling and place baking powder biscuits on top for something more cobbler-esque.

BRAISED TRIPE
VICTORIA REYNOLDS

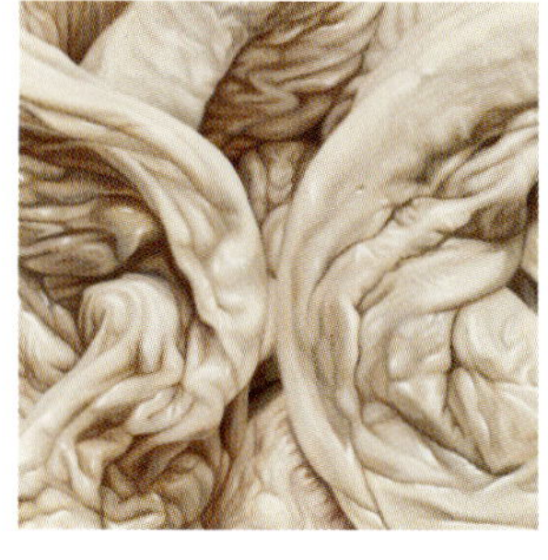

Tripe is not the easiest dish to sell: it's stomach lining, usually from a cow, and the thought of eating this part of an animal is hateful to most individuals. Therefore I propose that in lieu of telling your guests what you're serving, just serve it. After having a generous helping of this incredibly flavorful and incredibly inexpensive dish, they'll follow you willingly into your next food adventure. Tripe can be found at most ethnic markets where it is pre-washed and scalded, though additional soaking overnight may be to your benefit. As tripe is rich with fat and gelatin, the gravy that you will end up with is flavorful and has a velveteen texture that will pair well with simple mashed potatoes, buttered noodles or polenta.

INGREDIENTS   Serving size: 6

1 c. chopped dates
1 tsp. baking powder
1 c. coarsely chopped walnuts
Slivered orange peel or maraschino cherries

1 c. sugar
1 tbs. flour
whipped cream
2 eggs, separated

DIRECTIONS

1 PREHEAT oven to 425 degrees. BUTTER and line a 9" square baking pan with parchment paper, greasing the parchment after applied. Set aside. BEAT together sugar and egg yolks until fluffy, light and almost the color of butter. The mixture should leave a thick ribbon when lifted from the bowl. Add dates, walnuts, flour and baking powder. Incorporate thoroughly.

2 BEAT egg whites until they form stiff peaks, taking care not to over-beat. The whites should be shiny and NEVER curdled. FOLD the egg whites into the egg yolk and date mixture.

3 SPREAD the batter into the pan and bake for 15 minutes. COOL on a rack, then run a knife around the edges of the pan to loosen the crumble. Turn the crumble out of the pan, remove the parchment lining and break the crumble into six pieces, dividing amongst dessert plates. TOP with whipped cream and orange peel or maraschino cherries.

INGREDIENTS   Serving size: 8

12 oz. pearl onions, blanched and peeled
2 ¾ c. plus 1 tbs. all-purpose flour, divided
16 oz. button mushrooms, clean and halved
9 oz. new potatoes, scrubbed and ½" cubes
3 medium leeks, sliced ¼" rounds, white and
    pale-green parts only
2 medium carrots, peeled and sliced ¼" rounds
    (buy with tops on for sweetness)
24 tbs. (3 sticks) chilled, unsalted butter, divided

2 bunches fresh thyme
Juice of 1 lemon, or to taste
1 celery stalk, cut into thirds
4 c. homemade chicken stock
1 tbs. whole black peppercorns
2 tbs. flat-leaf parsley, chopped
1 large yellow onion, cut in half
8 oz. Parmigiano-Reggiano cheese
½ tsp. freshly ground black pepper

1 c. milk
1 tsp. sugar
1 4-lb. chicken
Zest of 3 lemons
3 large egg yolks
4 dried bay leaves
1 tbs. heavy cream
2 ¼ tsp. kosher salt

DIRECTIONS

1 COMBINE the chicken, chicken stock, yellow onion, bay leaves, peppercorns, ¼ of the thyme sprigs, and celery in a stockpot, and add enough water to cover. Bring the pot to a boil, reduce heat, and SIMMER uncovered for 1 hour.

2 PICK enough thyme leaves to equal five generous tbs.; set aside. In a food processor, PULVERIZE the parmesan cheese. Add 2 ½ c. flour, ¼ tsp. salt, and 1 tbs. thyme leaves to the cheese mixture. Pulse to incorporate. Cut 16 tbs of chilled butter into small cubes. Add to the dry ingredients and PULSE until mixture resembles coarse meal. While the food processor is running, add about 6 tbs. of ice water and 2 egg yolks until the dough holds together. Turn the dough out onto plastic wrap, flatten into a circle, and wrap well. CHILL at least one hour.

3 DRAIN the chicken and vegetables discarding the vegetable solids but reserving the stock. After the chicken is cool enough to handle, remove the skin; discard. Next, remove all the chicken meat from the carcass and SHRED into bite-size strips; set aside. Strain the stock through cheesecloth. Set aside 2 c. of the stock. Save remaining stock for another use (it will keep for about 2 months in the freezer).
PREHEAT oven to 375 degrees. MELT the remaining 8 tbs. butter in a large sauté pan or dutch oven over medium-high heat. Add red potatoes and pearl onions. SAUTE

4 about 5 minutes, stirring occasionally, until potatoes begin to turn golden. Add leeks, carrots, and mushrooms; cook 5 more minutes. Add remaining ¼ c. plus 1 tbs. flour, stirring continuously for 1 minute. Add reserved chicken stock and milk and bring to a SIMMER stirring constantly until thick and bubbly, about 2 to 3 minutes. NOTE: Make sure to scrape the bottom of your pan as the four will adhere to the hot pan, and nobody likes burnt gravy! Add chicken meat, parsley, remaining 2 tsp. of thyme, lemon zest, lemon juice, remaining 2 tsp. of salt, and pepper. TRANSFER mixture to an ovenproof casserole dish and set aside.

5 ROLL out the dough until it is ¼ inch thick. Transfer to a baking sheet and refrigerate, allowing the dough to CHILL 15 minutes. In a small bowl, whisk together the remaining yolk and heavy cream to create an egg wash. PLACE the dough over the top of the chicken mixture, tucking the extra dough around the edges, cutting slits into the crust to allow steam to escape. BRUSH the crust with the egg wash. Place finished pot pie on a baking sheet to avoid overspill. BAKE 40 to 45 minutes.

INGREDIENTS   Serving size: 6

1 bunch flat leaf parsley
6 garlic cloves, thinly sliced
Freshly grated parmesan cheese
1 qt. chicken stock (homemade preferred)
5 tomatoes, seeded (juice reserved), diced
1 ½ lbs. honeycomb tripe, rinsed, sliced thin
½ tsp. piment d'esplette (sub ⅛ tsp. cayenne)

1 tsp. salt
4 tbs. butter
3 bay leaves
1 c. diced carrot
1 c. diced celery
¼ lb. pancetta, diced
1 c. diced yellow onion

DIRECTIONS

1 MELT the butter in a dutch oven or heavy stock pot over low heat. ADD the celery, carrots, onion and pancetta. COOK for about 10 minutes until vegetables are wilted. The mixture should just barely begin to turn golden brown.

2 ADD the bay leaves, tomatoes, garlic, salt, piment d'esplette (or cayenne), tripe, reserved tomato juice and chicken stock to the pot. Raise the heat and bring to a slow boil. Reduce the heat to a slow, even simmer. COVER the pot and cook for two hours.
CHECK the consistency of the tripe. It should be smooth and when you bite into it, there should be no resistance. If the tripe is not done, continue to SIMMER until the tripe reaches desired tenderness.

3 STRAIN the solids from the pot once the tripe is ready. Discard the bay leaves and leave the gravy in the pot. Increase the heat to medium-high and simmer. REDUCE the gravy by half until it is the consistency of heavy cream. When the gravy thickens, re-introduce the tripe and vegetable mixture to the pot.

4 SERVE the braised tripe over potatoes or simple buttered noodles. GARNISH with parsley and parmesan. Add freshly ground black pepper for enhanced flavor.

PECAN PIE WITH SPICED CRUST
JENNIFER RUBELL

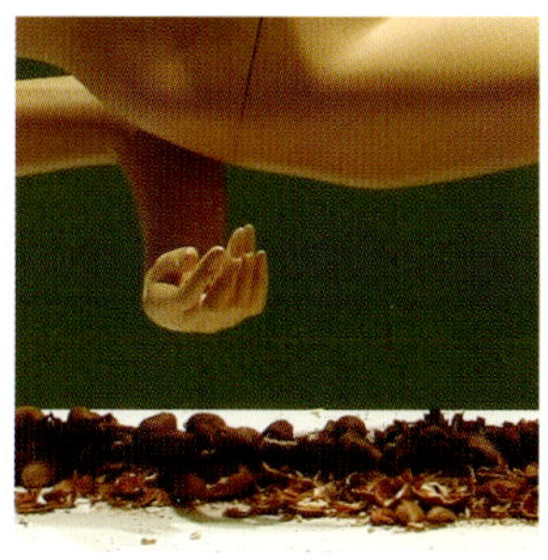

I love pie crust. Now, butter reigns supreme for flavor, therefore you will not find shortening listed in the ingredients. It is terribly important to keep your pie dough cool; the chilled butter will ensure that you are supplied with ample layers of delectable, crisp and unctuous crust that are the perfect accompaniment to a pie as rich as this. Buy your pecans from a location that has quick turnover—nuts are high in oil and therefore spoil quickly. If you really want to impress, order your pecans from one of many sellers from Texas or Georgia, where gargantuan pecans not only steal the show but provide maximum flavor.

MUSHROOM RISOTTO OF FARRO WITH HERB PESTO AND RABBIT
GREG STEWART

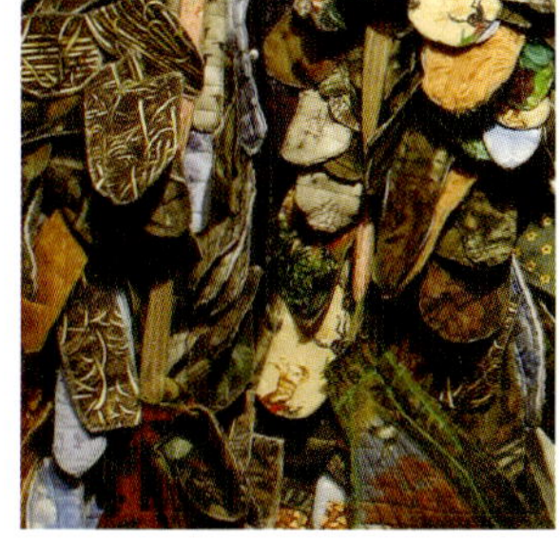

While one doesn't always associate farro with risotto, it's a great change of pace from Arborio or Carnaroli rice. It is chewier, has excellent texture, and can you imagine the fiber! This is a great, meaty dish but can also be made vegetarian. In place of rabbit or chicken stock, vegetable stock may be substituted, however in my experience, a well rounded meat stock brings so much to the table where risotto is concerned.

LAYERED VEGETABLE TORTE
TATTFOO TAN

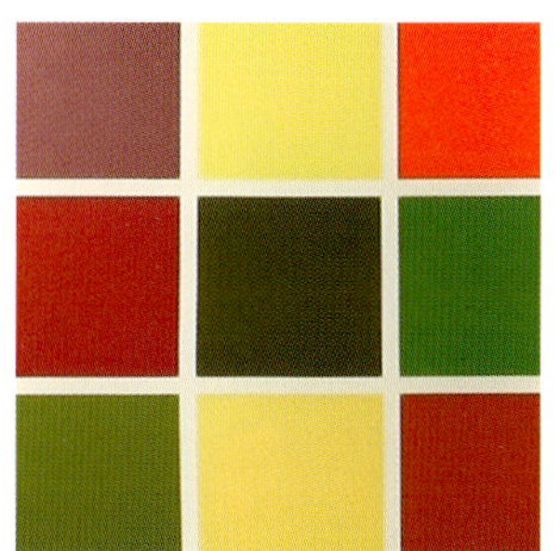

You don't need to be a vegetarian to enjoy this delicious torte, which celebrates all the color and magnificence that the vegetable garden has to offer. The fact that it has a goodly amount of bread crumbs on the outside, half of it is fried, and looks stunning on a platter will entice everyone to take a bite. Plus when sliced into, beautiful and colorful striations catch the eye. Serve with some delicious couscous to sop up any leaking juices and with a dab or two of room-temperature goat cheese; this will delight the palate. If you hate them (as so many do) omit the beets… but they're quite good with this.

INGREDIENTS   Serving size: 6

The Pie Crust
¼ tsp. salt
1 large egg
3 tbs. sugar
½ tsp. cinnamon
¼ tsp. ground clove
1 c. all-purpose flour
¼ tsp. baking powder
¼ tsp. freshly grated nutmeg
4 tbs. unsalted butter, chilled, cubed small

The Pie Filling
¾ c. sugar
3 large eggs
6 tbs. butter
Pinch of salt
1 c. dark corn syrup
2 c. (about ½ lb.) pecan halves
2 tbs. good bourbon (plus a glass for yourself)

DIRECTIONS

1 DOUGH | In the bowl of a food processor, PULSE all dry ingredients. Add butter and pulse until the mixture resembles coarse meal. Beat the egg with a fork and add to the butter mixture, pulsing until the mixture just comes together. Place the mixture onto a floured work surface or cutting board and knead 4 or 5 times until the dough is smooth. FORM the dough into a disk and refrigerate for 1 hour. Roll out the dough to a ⅛" thick disc and transfer to a 9" pie dish, crimping the edges to your liking. (When I make a pie, I never worry: if my "end product" looks like a 4 year old made it, I simply say that my dessert is rustic! I suggest you do the same.) Once the pie shell is formed, throw it into the refrigerator to chill (at least 30 minutes).

2 FILLING | Combine the corn syrup and sugar in a saucepan and STIR to mix. Place over low heat and bring to a boil without stirring - swirl the pan by the handle if you feel that the contents need to be agitated. Remove from heat. Add the butter and allow it to melt. In a separate mixing bowl, thoroughly WHISK the eggs, adding pinch of salt and the bourbon (not yours, of course). DRIZZLE the syrup into the bowl with the eggs, whisking to combine. Work slowly - you don't want scrambled eggs in your pie and the heat of the syrup will still be quite hot.

3 PREHEAT the oven to 350 degrees. In your chilled pie crust, place the pecans in single layer, then POUR the custard mixture over the pecans. Make sure the pecans are coated with the custard by pushing them down with a fork or spoon to prevent burning.

4 BAKE on the the bottom rack of the oven for 45 minutes or until the crust is golden and the filling is set. It will be slightly jiggly and puffed in the center. COOL on a rack. Serve warm or at room temperature. A dollop of spiced whipped cream, or whipped cream slightly sweetened and flavored with additional bourbon work well as options for pie toppings.

INGREDIENTS   Serving size: 4

¾ c. walnuts, toasted
1 c. fresh flat-leaf parsley
¾ c. dried porcini mushrooms
½ c. shaved parmesan cheese
6 c. rabbit stock (sub chicken stock)
Kosher salt and black pepper to taste
1 lb. cooked rabbit meat (sub chicken meat)
24 oz. assorted fresh wild mushrooms, stemmed

2 c. farro
¾ c. olive oil
½ stick butter
3 garlic cloves
1 c. fresh basil
¾ c. dry white wine
White pepper to taste

DIRECTIONS

1 PESTO | In the bowl of a processor, PULSE the walnuts until coarsely ground. Add the basil, parsley and garlic to the bowl. Add salt and pepper to taste. Pulse until a paste forms. DRIZZLE the oil in a steady stream to finish the pesto. Set aside.
MELT butter over medium heat, in a heavy sauce pan, and SUATE the mushrooms until golden brown. Season with salt and pepper. Set aside.

2 RISOTTO | In a Dutch Oven, add the farro, porcini mushrooms, and 2 c. of stock to a BOIL. Reduce your heat to medium-high and cook until the liquid is nearly absorbed. Continue to COOK the farro mixture, adding a ladle full of stock at a time, cooking until the liquid is nearly absorbed before adding more liquid. This may take 30 minutes. It is not necessary to stir constantly, but do stir every few minutes and keep your eye on the pot.

3 CHECK your risotto for doneness once you are finished incorporating the rabbit stock. If it is too al dente, add more stock or water and continue to cook until the risotto is as soft as you prefer. Remember that farro has more texture than traditional rice and will not be as soft when cooked.
Off the heat, stir in ½ of the pesto, cooked rabbit and sautéed mushrooms. Plate and garnish with an additional dollop of pesto and a few shavings of fresh parmesan cheese. SPRINKLE with white pepper, which will add depth to the rabbit and mushrooms without harshness

INGREDIENTS   Serving size: 10

3 yellow bell peppers
Salt and pepper, to taste
3 tablespoons butter, soft
8 roma tomatoes, sliced in half
1 bunch marjoram, stripped (buds and leaves reserved)
½ cup panko bread crumbs (semi-coarse dried crumbs)

6 zucchini
4 large beets
3 red bell peppers
Olive oil for frying
1 large sweet potato
3 to 4 large eggplant

DIRECTIONS

1 PREHEAT oven to 375 degrees. Generously butter a 10" springform pan and distribute the panko evenly over the bottom and sides, covering completely. Set aside.
POUR oil into a sauté pan or skillet to a 1" depth and heat to 350 degrees. SLICE the tops off of the eggplant and cut into 1/8" thick, lengthwise slices. Repeat this with the zucchini and sweet potato. FRY the vegetable slices in the oil a few at a time until they are lightly browned.
Over an open flame, CHAR the yellow and red peppers until blackened on all sides; remove from heat, and seal in plastic wrap to steam. Once they're cool enough to handle, REMOVE from the plastic wrap and gently rub the peppers to remove the charred skin. RINSE under water to remove any seeds or ribs. Slice and set aside.

2 PLACE tomatoes on a baking pan and coat liberally with olive oil, salt, and pepper. COAT beets with olive oil, salt and pepper; wrap each beet in foil. Roast the beets and tomatoes together for about 1 hr. When done, the tomatoes should appear almost dry, though with some moisture left; when the beets are done, they should slice easily with a sharp knife. Cool, peel and slice the beets into 1/8" rounds. DRAIN tomatoes in a colander. Set both aside.

3 ASSEMBLE the torte by taking the eggplant and fanning the slices in a decorative pattern along the bottom of the springform pan. Work your way up the sides of the pan in a single layer, overlapping as necessary. Continue adding eggplant slices until they come over the top edge of your pan. SEASON the layer with salt and pepper. Layer remaining vegetables in the following order: yellow bell pepper, sweet potato, red bell pepper, roasted tomato, zucchini and beet. Between each layer, strew a few marjoram leaves and buds. Salt and pepper to taste. FOLD the overhanging eggplant over the beets. Layer with remaining eggplant. SPRINKLE additional bread crumbs over the top.

4 BAKE at 375 degrees until browned and the torte is bubbling around the edges. Carefully invert the torte onto a plate or cakestand and release it from the springform pan. SERVE immediatly. To serve later, compress with a heavy plate. Chill for at least 4 hrs., invert the torte and serve.

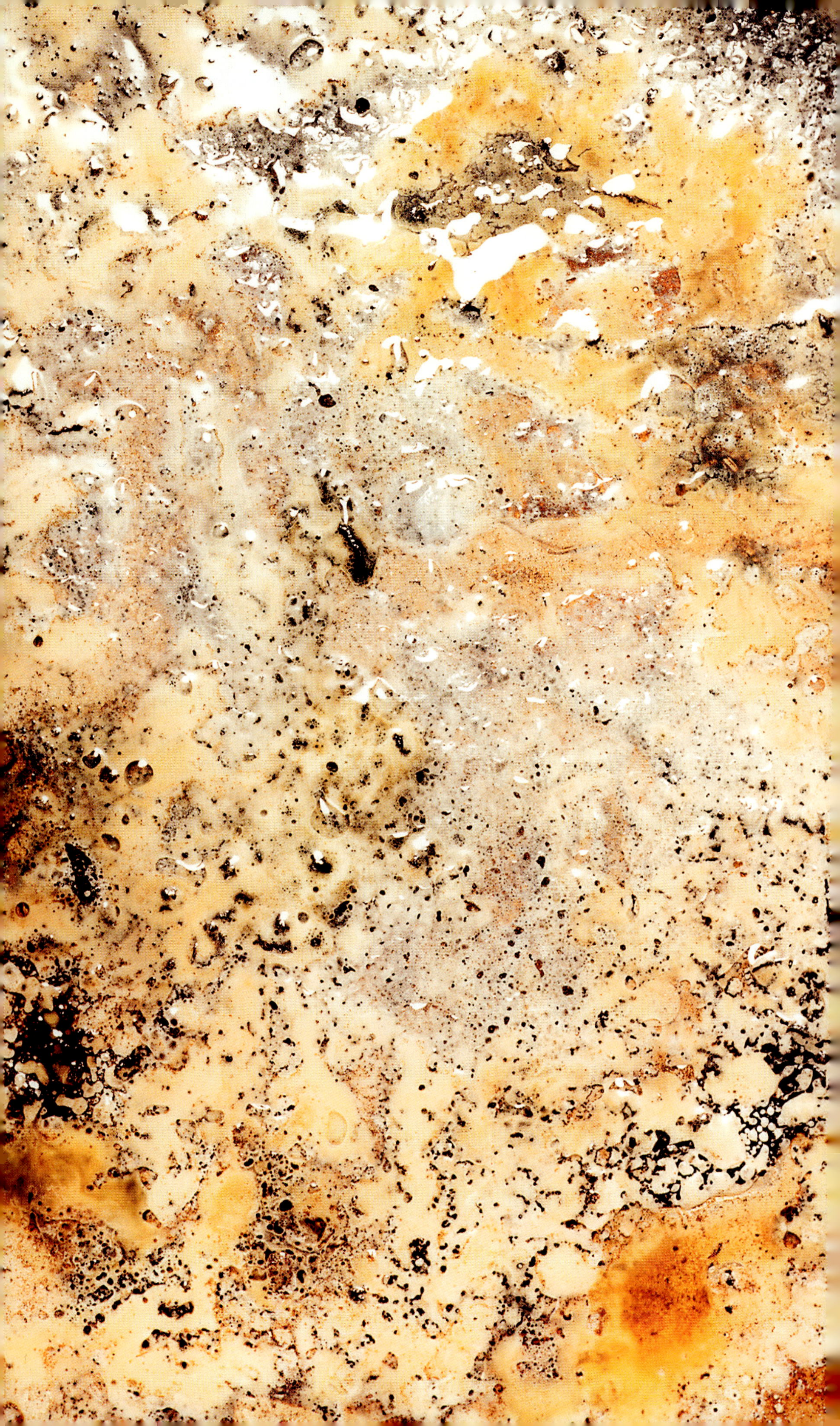

ARTIST PROFILES

TIM BERG AND REBEKAH MYERS

Timothy Berg and Rebekah Myers are a multimedia studio art collaborative based in Claremont, California. Berg and Myers create sculpture and installations that employ humor and metaphor to simultaneously disarm the viewer and challenge them to address humankind's propensity for making things disappear. Although seemingly lighthearted and fun, *Here Today, Gone Tomorrow* wryly comments on our culture's insatiable appetite and the consequences of over-consuming. Currently Berg is an Assistant Professor at Pitzer College and Myers is a full-time studio artist in Claremont, California.

Pages 22-23
myersbergstudios.com

SITA KURATOMI BHAUMIK

Sita Kuratomi Bhaumik is an artist who likes to think of her work as the lovechild of Edward Said and Willy Wonka. An interdisciplinary artist, educator, and writer born and raised in the suburbs of Los Angeles to Indian and Japanese Colombian parents, she moved to the Bay Area after receiving her B.A., cum laude, in studio art from Scripps College. She also holds an M.F.A. from California College of the Arts and an M.A. in visual and critical studies. Bhaumik has collaborated with organizations such as APICC, SomArts, 18 Reasons, 826 Valencia, The Asian Art Museum of San Francisco, and Yerba Buena Center for the Arts. She has been the art features editor for *Hyphen* magazine and a board member and programming committee chair for Kearny Street Workshop. She also teaches photography and portfolio development at RayKo Photo Center. Bhaumik lives and works in the San Francisco Bay Area.

Pages 24-27, endpage (front)
sitabhaumik.com

SHANNON HAYES FASELER

Originally from Texas, Shannon Faseler studied at the Art Institute of Chicago, receiving her M.F.A in drawing and painting. About her current work, Faseler states, "What is so interesting to me is the pathology of an organism that completely consumes and alters the environment it occupies on a microscopic level..." Inspired by the aftermath of Hurricane Katrina in New Orleans, Faseler's installation investigates the visual properties of mold growth in food and houses. She currently lives in Southern California and was selected for Laguna Art Museum's 2010 OsCene exhibition featuring emerging California artists.

Pages 28-31
shannonfaseler.com

DUSTIN WAYNE HARRIS

Dustin Wayne Harris was born in Brunswick, Georgia, in 1982, and raised in Tustin, California. In 2007, Harris graduated from the School of Visual Arts, New York. His work has been shown at Nicole Klagsbrun Gallery and Heist Gallery, both in New York. Harris has been nominated twice for the prestigious Tiffany Grant. Most recently, Harris presented his work entitled "A New Career in a New Town" at the Art Production Fund LAB, a non-profit organization dedicated to facilitating new and ambitious projects by contemporary artists. Harris currently lives in Astoria, New York.

Pages 32-34, 75

PAMELA MICHELLE JOHNSON

Raised in California, Pamela Johnson graduated from California Polytechnic State University, San Luis Obispo, with a B.S. in civil engineering and an art minor with honors. After graduation, she continued to pursue art independently while working as an engineer in the construction industry. In 2003, Johnson decided to focus on art as a career, uprooting from her native California to live in Chicago. She has exhibited her work in galleries and museums through out Chicago and the United States. Her most recent body of work, *American Still Life*, has been featured in numerous magazines, papers, and online publications. She lives and works in Chicago.

Pages 35-37
www.pamelamichellejohnson.com

JENNIFER L. KNOX

Poet and fiction writer Jennifer L. Knox altered this Mark Bittman cookbook as a wedding present for friends with a black marker, glue and paper to include her own witty introduction. Her poems have appeared in four volumes of *The Best American Poetry* series, *Great American Prose Poems: From Poe to Present*, and numerous publications such as *The New Yorker* and *American Poetry Review*.

Pages 38-39
jenniferlknox.com

MARY PARISI

Mary Parisi was born and raised in San Francisco. She holds an M.A. in sculpture from San Francisco State University and an M.F.A. in photography from the San Francisco Art Institute. Parisi's work has been shown nationally and internationally, including JK Gallery, Los Angeles, Fotobild, Berlin, and the Lishui Photo Festival, Lishui, China, with a solo exhibition at the Houston Center for Photography. In 2006, her photographs were published in *Photonews*. Parisi has exhibited throughout the United States, Germany and China. Her work is collected by the Museum of FIne Arts, Houston, and the Museum of Photography in Lishui, China. She lives and works in the San Francisco Bay Area.

Pages 4, 40-43, 75, 80
maryparisi.com

JUSTIN PERRICONE

Justin Perricone is a graphic designer with a penchant for typography, layout, and identity, all with a sprinkling of minimalism. His work has been featured on *BoingBoing* and *Bon Appetit*. He's also a photographer, writer, blogger, food junkie, and budding homebrewer. Justin lives with his wife Dorie in Cambridge, Massachusetts.

Pages 44-45
perriconedesign.com

VICTORIA REYNOLDS

Los Angeles-based artist Victoria Reynolds paints luscious and sensual renderings of meat that are often characterized as both fascinating and repulsive, while also referencing historical sixteenth- and seventeenth-century still-life paintings. Flesh as a subject matter alludes to all animals, including humans, and our inter-connectedness. Reynolds exhibits internationally and has been featured in *ArtForum*, *Art in America,* and *Frieze*. Recently, she has created a new body of work of abstracted vegetable and fruit imagery.

Pages 46-48, 75
richardhellergallery.com/dynamic/artist.asp?ArtistID=30

JENNIFER RUBELL

Jennifer Rubell received a B.A. in fine arts from Harvard University and subsequently attended the Culinary Institute of America. Some of Rubell's notable previous projects include *Old-Fashioned*, at the Los Angeles County Museum of Art; The de Pury Diptych at the Saatchi Gallery, London; *Icons*, at the Brooklyn Museum; *Creation*, for Performa, the New York performance-art festival; and, since 2001, a yearly breakfast project in the courtyard of the Rubell Family Collection in Miami during Art Basel Miami Beach. She wrote about food for over a decade prior to beginning her artistic practice, including columns in the *Miami Herald* and *Domino* magazine, and the book *Real Life Entertaining* (Harper Collins). Rubell lives in New York City.

Pages 49-51, 77
jenniferrubell.com

STEPHEN j SHANABROOK

Stephen j Shanabrook was born in Cleveland, Ohio, in 1965. He received his B.F.A. from Syracuse University and also studied in Florence, Italy. His residencies include Skowhegan School of Painting and Sculpture and De Atelier in The Netherlands. In collaboration with Veronika Georgieva, Shanabrook has created advertising campaigns for fashion label Comme des Garçons and for the Saatchi and Saatchi advertising agency. His work has been shown at Drawing Center, New York; Swiss Institute, New York; and the Moscow Biennale and is part of many public and private collections in the U.S and abroad, including Damien Hirst's "murderme" collection and the Museum of Old and New Art, Tasmania. Shanabrook resides in New York.

Pages 52-55
stephenshanabrook.com

GREG STEWART

Greg Stewart, mulitmedia artist, lives and works in Virginia. Stewart's work stems from an interest in geography, more specifically, human geography, the study of how we situate or arrange ourselves in the world. His work investigates aspects of mobility: mobility as a physical operation, a metaphorical gesture, and as a spark for things that drive our imaginations. Stewart's recent work involves the invention of complex structures and absurd situations that offer imaginary solutions to migration and survival. Stewart's work has been exhibited widely both nationally and internationally. His *On The Edge Is Decorated With Carvings* performance and installation was completed during his residency at CSUF Begovich Gallery and CSUF Grand Central Art Center. This piece imagines the future of sustainability and agriculture within an urban context, a world of genetic modification where pigs grow produce and our gardens become mobile.

Stewart's has an M.F.A. in sculpture from Ohio University and is currently an associate professor of sculpture at James Madison University.

Pages 56-59, 77
Photographs by Angelica Perez
gregstewartsite.org

TATTFOO TAN

Tattfoo Tan is a self-taught, New York-based artist whose work addresses community and sustainability. Much of his work seeks to merge art and life and inspire group participation. *Nature Matching System* is a reminder to consume your daily recommended doses of color. Each colored square is matched to the skin color of a fruit or vegetable. They get many of their colors from phytonutrients, compounds that play key roles in health and reduce the risk of heart disease and cancer. The more colors come together at a meal, the better. Tan has been featured in the *New York Times* and *Eat Me Daily* and received an award for public design from the City of New York for the rehabilitation of the Bronx River Art Center.

Pages 60-62, 77
tattfoo.com

ACKNOWLEDGMENTS & THANKS

DEAN, COLLEGE OF THE ARTS
Dr. Joseph H. Arnold, Jr.

CHAIR, DEPARTMENT OF ART
Dana Lamb

DIRECTOR, NICHOLAS & LEE BEGOVICH GALLERY
Mike McGee

ASSISTANT TO THE DIRECTOR
Jacqueline Bunge
Marilyn Moore

GALLERY TECHNICIAN
Martin Lorigan

GALLERY ASSISTANTS
Drü Biba
S.A. Hawkins
Kimberly Mckinnis
Martha Rocha

EXHIBITION CURATORS
Alyssa Cordova and Heather Richards-Siddons

EXHIBITION DESIGN STUDENTS
Lara Camagni • Cassandra Erb • Jennifer Frias • Loriann Hernandez • Linda Iwasaki • Lilia Lamas • Martin Lorigan Joanne Mace • Kimberly Mckinnis • Martha Rocha Concepcion Rodriguez • Wendy Sherman • Allison Town Emily Darman Allen Tyler

CATALOG PRODUCTION
ESSAYISTS
Nicole Caruth
Megan Fizell

CATALOG CREATIVE DIRECTOR
Theron Moore

SENIOR DESIGNER
Laurel Webster

DESIGNERS
Rodrigo Calderon
Ashley Sinohui

ANNOUNCEMENT CONCEPT
Rodrigo Calderon
Ashley Sinohui
Laurel Webster

ANNOUNCEMENT DESIGN
Rodrigo Calderon

POSTER DESIGN
Rodrigo Calderon

PHOTOGRAPHY
Sita Kuratomi Bhaumik
Alyssa Cordova
Kurt Simonson
Michael Quinn (pages 25, 28, 30, 37, 58-61, 64-66, 77)

EDITOR
Sue Henger

PRINTER
Permanent Printing Limited, Hong Kong, China

TYPEFACES
Serifa
Modern
Acquired Script

EXHIBITION & PROGRAMMING SPONSORS
Cal State Fullerton Art Alliance

LIFE MEMBERS
Nicholas and Lee Begovich and Patricia Dolson

DONORS
Gene and Shirley Laroff • William and Joyce Leong
Dr. Martin and Suzanne Serbin • Carol Wakeman

PATRONS
Floyd and Maxine Allen • Drs. Joseph and Voiza Arnold
Lois Austin • Renauld and Martha Bartholomew
Drs. Thomas and Carol Beardmore • Dr. Herbert and
Marilyn Benson • Gary and Lynn Chalupsky • John and
Janice DeLoof • Jean Fischer • Nancy Fix • Leonard and
Sylvia Garber • Tallya Geiger • Drs. Milton Gordon and
Margaret Faulwell Bill and Milly Heaton • Ginny Kadau
Peggy Martin • Sylvia Meluzin • Charlotte Oliva Roberto
Cheryl Quadrelli • J. Brenton Shore • Margaret Starks
David and Cathrynn Thorsen • Lorraine Walkington

ARTISTS
Timothy Berg & Rebekah Myers
Sita Kuratomi Bhaumik
Shannon Hayes Faseler
Dustin Wayne Harris
Pamela Michelle Johnson
Jennifer L. Knox
Mary Parisi
Justin Perricone
Victoria Reynolds
Jennifer Rubell
Stephen j Shanabrook
Greg Stewart
Tattfoo Tan

THANKS TO
Arts Inter Club Council • Associated Students, Inc.
California State University, Fullerton, College of the Arts
CSUF Department of Visual Arts • CSUF College of the Arts,
Marketing and Patron Services • Associated Students, Inc.
Backyard in a Jar • Exhibition Design 453 A/B students
Fullerton Arboretum • Grand Central Art Center,
Artist in Residence Program • James Madison University
PEO of Riverside • Sixpack Projects
Society of Museum Associates

SPECIAL THANKS
Jim and Cynde Adler of Adler & Co. Gallery
Gustavo Arellano • Harriet Bouldin • Mylan Chacon
Jason Chakravarty • Noelle Cordova • Pete Deeble
Gerry Donnelly • Jonathan Dye • Ciara Ennis
Gillian Ferguson • Krystal Glasman • Darra Goldstein
Terry Goodman • Lora Gramberg • Joanna Grasso
Charla Hall • Deborah Hawekotte and Richard Heller
of Richard Heller Gallery • Pam Ingersoll • Elizabeth Thacker
Jones Caitlin Keller • Linda Kenny • Anna McGarvey
Gary Mecija • Angelica Perez • Ruth Phaneuf of Nicole
Klagsbrun • Gretchen Potts • Jeff Rau Ward and Marlene Rau
Gloria Robbins • Veronika Shanabrook • Andrea Sims
Delilah Snell • Dan and Lois Stentz • Stephen Freidman Gallery

We would like to thank our families, friends, co-workers and
colleagues who supported and encouraged us throughout this
process. An extra special thanks to our loving and ever-patient
husbands, David Cordova and Brent Siddons, without whom
none of this would be possible.

Published in conjunction with the exhibition
Acquired Taste: Food and the Art of Consumption
October 29-December 11, 2011
Participating Artists © 2012
Nicholas & Lee Begovich Gallery
California State University Fullerton
800 North State College Blvd.
Fullerton, CA 92834
www.arts.fullerton.edu
www.acquiredtaste.sixpackprojects.com

ISBN: 978-0-935314-82-3

Endpage photo, front: Sita Bhaumik
Endpage photo, back: Kurt Simonson
Page 4, 80: Mary Parisi

Printed in Hong Kong

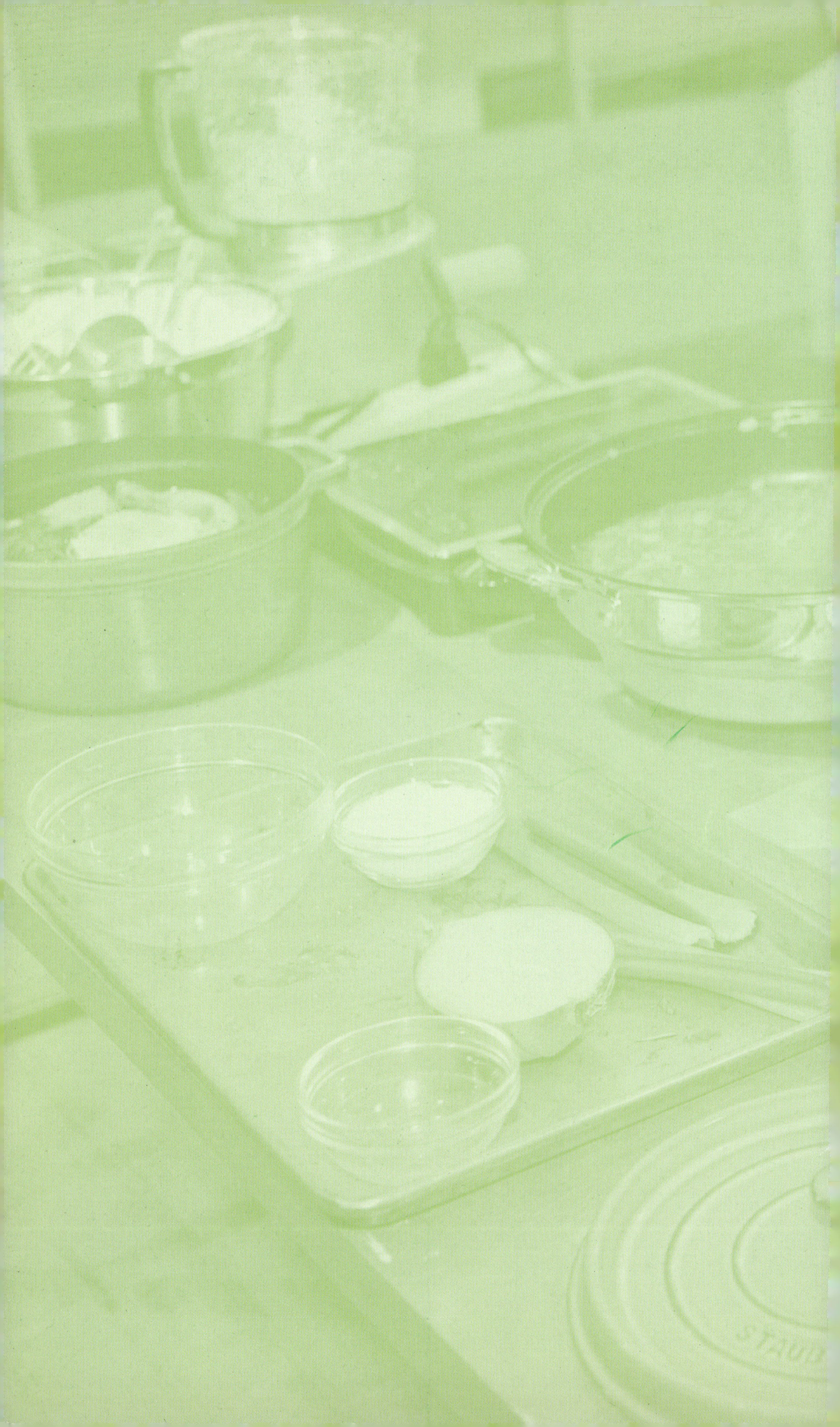